# Agnes de Mille

# Agnes de Mille

## MARGARET SPEAKER-YUAN

CHELSEA HOUSE PUBLISHERS

NEW YORK · PHILADELPHIA

**Chelsea House Publishers**
EDITOR-IN-CHIEF  Nancy Toff
EXECUTIVE EDITOR  Remmel T. Nunn
MANAGING EDITOR  Karyn Gullen Browne
COPY CHIEF  Juliann Barbato
PICTURE EDITOR  Adrian G. Allen
ART DIRECTOR  Maria Epes
MANUFACTURING MANAGER  Gerald Levine

**American Women of Achievement**
SENIOR EDITOR  Constance Jones

**Staff for AGNES DE MILLE**
TEXT EDITOR  Marian W. Taylor
DEPUTY COPY CHIEF  Nicole Bowen
EDITORIAL ASSISTANTS  Claire Wilson and Judith Weinstein
PICTURE RESEARCHERS  Joan Beard and Diana Gongora
ASSISTANT ART DIRECTOR  Loraine Machlin
DESIGNER Debora Smith
PRODUCTION MANAGER  Joseph Romano
PRODUCTION COORDINATOR  Marie Claire Cebrián
COVER ART  Bryn Barnard
COVER ORNAMENT  Excerpt from labanotation score of *Rodeo*,
            courtesy of the Dance Labanotation Bureau

3  5  7  9  8  6  4  2

Library of Congress Cataloging-in-Publication Data

Speaker-Yuan, Margaret.
  Agnes de Mille.

(American women of achievement)
Bibliography: p.
Includes index.
Summary: Traces the life and accomplishments of the choreog-
rapher, dancer, and author who created ballets based on Ameri-
can themes and choreographed the musical *Oklahoma!*
ISBN 1-55546-648-6
      0-7910-0430-9 (pbk.)
1. De Mille, Agnes.   2. Dancers—United States—
Biography.   3. Choreographers—United States—Biography.
[1. De Mille, Agnes. 2. Dancers. 3. Choreographers]  I. Title.
II. Series.
GV1785.D36Y8   1988       792.8'2'0924 [B] [92]       87-30949

# CONTENTS

# AMERICAN WOMEN OF ACHIEVEMENT

Abigail Adams
*women's rights advocate*

Jane Addams
*social worker*

Louisa May Alcott
*author*

Marian Anderson
*singer*

Susan B. Anthony
*woman suffragist*

Ethel Barrymore
*actress*

Clara Barton
*founder of the American
Red Cross*

Elizabeth Blackwell
*physician*

Nellie Bly
*journalist*

Margaret Bourke-White
*photographer*

Pearl Buck
*author*

Rachel Carson
*biologist and author*

Mary Cassatt
*artist*

Agnes de Mille
*choreographer*

Emily Dickinson
*poet*

Isadora Duncan
*dancer*

Amelia Earhart
*aviator*

Mary Baker Eddy
*founder of the Christian
Science church*

Betty Friedan
*feminist*

Althea Gibson
*tennis champion*

Emma Goldman
*political activist*

Helen Hayes
*actress*

Lillian Hellman
*playwright*

Katharine Hepburn
*actress*

Karen Horney
*psychoanalyst*

Anne Hutchinson
*religious leader*

Mahalia Jackson
*gospel singer*

Helen Keller
*humanitarian*

Jeane Kirkpatrick
*diplomat*

Emma Lazarus
*poet*

Clare Boothe Luce
*author and diplomat*

Barbara McClintock
*biologist*

Margaret Mead
*anthropologist*

Edna St. Vincent Millay
*poet*

Julia Morgan
*architect*

Grandma Moses
*painter*

Louise Nevelson
*sculptor*

Sandra Day O'Connor
*Supreme Court justice*

Georgia O'Keeffe
*painter*

Eleanor Roosevelt
*diplomat and humanitarian*

Wilma Rudolph
*champion athlete*

Florence Sabin
*medical researcher*

Beverly Sills
*opera singer*

Gertrude Stein
*author*

Gloria Steinem
*feminist*

Harriet Beecher Stowe
*author and abolitionist*

Mae West
*entertainer*

Edith Wharton
*author*

Phillis Wheatley
*poet*

Babe Didrikson Zaharias
*champion athlete*

CHELSEA HOUSE PUBLISHERS

# "REMEMBER THE LADIES"

## MATINA S. HORNER

Remember the Ladies." That is what Abigail Adams wrote to her husband, John, then a delegate to the Continental Congress, as the Founding Fathers met in Philadelphia to form a new nation in March of 1776. "Be more generous and favorable to them than your ancestors. Do not put such unlimited power in the hands of the Husbands. If particular care and attention is not paid to the Ladies," Abigail Adams warned, "we are determined to foment a Rebellion, and will not hold ourselves bound by any Laws in which we have no voice, or Representation."

The words of Abigail Adams, one of the earliest American advocates of women's rights, were prophetic. Because when we have not "remembered the ladies," they have, by their words and deeds, reminded us so forcefully of the omission that we cannot fail to remember them. For the history of American women is as interesting and varied as the history of our nation as a whole. American women have played an integral part in founding, settling, and building our country. Some we remember as remarkable women who—against great odds—achieved distinction in the public arena: Anne Hutchinson, who in the 17th century became a charismatic religious leader; Phillis Wheatley, an 18th-century black slave who became a poet; Susan B. Anthony, whose name is synonymous with the 19th-century women's rights movement and who led the struggle to enfranchise women; and, in our own century, Amelia Earhart, the first woman to cross the Atlantic Ocean by air.

These extraordinary women certainly merit our admiration, but other women, "common women," many of them all but forgotten, should also be recognized for their contributions to American thought and culture. Women have been community builders; they have founded schools and formed voluntary associations to help those in need; they have assumed the major responsibility for rearing children, passing on from one generation to the next the values that keep a culture alive. These and innumerable other contributions, once ignored, are now being recognized by scholars, students, and the public. It is exciting and gratifying to realize that a part of our history that was hardly acknowledged a few generations ago is now being studied and brought to light.

In recent decades, the field of women's history has grown from obscurity to a politically controversial splinter movement to academic respectability, in many cases mainstreamed into such traditional disciplines as history, economics, and psychology. Scholars of women, both female and male, have organized research centers at such prestigious institutions as Wellesley College, Stanford University, and the University of California. Other notable centers for women's studies are the Center for the American Woman and Politics at the Eagleton Institute of Politics at Rutgers University; the Henry A. Murray Research Center for the Study of Lives, at Radcliffe College; and the Women's Research and Education Institute, the research arm of the Congressional Caucus on Women's Issues. Other scholars and public figures have established archives and libraries, such as the Schlesinger Library on the History of Women in America, at Radcliffe College, and the Sophia Smith Collection, at Smith College, to collect and preserve the written and tangible legacies of women.

From the initial donation of the Women's Rights Collection in 1943, the Schlesinger Library grew to encompass vast collections documenting the manifold accomplishments of American women. Simultaneously, the women's movement in general and the academic discipline of women's studies in particular also began with a narrow definition and gradually expanded their mandate. Early causes such as woman suffrage and social reform, abolition and organized labor were joined by newer concerns such as the history of women in business and the professions and in politics and government; the study of the family; and social issues such as health policy and education.

Women, as historian Arthur M. Schlesinger, jr., once pointed out, "have constituted the most spectacular casualty of traditional history.

# INTRODUCTION

They have made up at least half the human race, but you could never tell that by looking at the books historians write." The new breed of historians is remedying that omission. They have written books about immigrant women and about working-class women who struggled for survival in cities and about black women who met the challenges of life in rural areas. They are telling the stories of women who, despite the barriers of tradition and economics, became lawyers and doctors and public figures.

The women's studies movement has also led scholars to question traditional interpretations of their respective disciplines. For example, the study of war has traditionally been an exercise in military and political analysis, an examination of strategies planned and executed by men. But scholars of women's history have pointed out that wars have also been periods of tremendous change and even opportunity for women, because the very absence of men on the home front enabled them to expand their educational, economic, and professional activities and to assume leadership in their homes.

The early scholars of women's history showed a unique brand of courage in choosing to investigate new subjects and take new approaches to old ones. Often, like their subjects, they endured criticism and even ostracism by their academic colleagues. But their efforts have unquestionably been worthwhile, because with the publication of each new study and book another piece of the historical patchwork is sewn into place, revealing an increasingly comprehensive picture of the role of women in our rich and varied history.

Such books on groups of women are essential, but books that focus on the lives of individuals are equally indispensable. Biographies can be inspirational, offering their readers the example of people with vision who have looked outside themselves for their goals and have often struggled against great obstacles to achieve them. Marian Anderson, for instance, had to overcome racial bigotry in order to perfect her art and perform as a concert singer. Isadora Duncan defied the rules of classical dance to find true artistic freedom. Jane Addams had to break down society's notions of the proper role for women in order to create new social institutions, notably the settlement house. All of these women had to come to terms both with themselves and with the world in which they lived. Only then could they move ahead as pioneers in their chosen callings.

Biography can inspire not only by adulation but also by realism. It helps us to see not only the qualities in others that we hope to emulate but also, perhaps, the weaknesses that made them "human." By helping us identify with the subject on a more personal level they help us to feel that we, too, can achieve such goals. We read about Eleanor Roosevelt, for example, who occupied a unique and seemingly enviable position as the wife of the president. Yet we can sympathize with her inner dilemma: an inherently shy woman who had to force herself to live a most public life in order to use her position to benefit others. We may not be able to imagine ourselves having the immense poetic talent of Emily Dickinson, but from her story we can understand the challenges faced by a creative woman who was expected to fulfill many family responsibilities. And though few of us will ever reach the level of athletic accomplishment displayed by Wilma Rudolph or Babe Zaharias, we can still appreciate their spirit, their overwhelming will to excel.

A biography is a multifaceted lens. It is first of all a magnification, the intimate examination of one particular life. But at the same time, it is a wide-angle lens, informing us about the world in which the subject lived. We come away from reading about one life knowing more about the social, political, and economic fabric of the time. It is for this reason, perhaps, that the great New England essayist Ralph Waldo Emerson wrote, in 1841, "There is properly no history: only biography." And it is also why biography, and particularly women's biography, will continue to fascinate writers and readers alike.

# Agnes
## de Mille

*Agnes de Mille plays the role of Cowgirl in* Rodeo, *the ground-breaking comic ballet she created for the Ballet Russe de Monte Carlo in 1942.*

# ONE

# Opening Night

Agnes de Mille whirled across the stage and slid to a stop. Counting the beats until her next cue, she watched the other dancers kick their way through the dress rehearsal of her new ballet, *Rodeo: The Courting at Burnt Ranch*. She breathed deeply, gathering strength for her next series of leaps.

A dress rehearsal calls for full costume, but on this Manhattan afternoon in October 1942, de Mille and her fellow dancers wore only plain black tights and practice leotards. Costumes for the ballet's premiere—by now only hours away—lay unfinished, heaped in the uptown apartment of costume maker Barbara Karinska. As she completed each section, the frantic Karinska sent it to the theater by taxi, but by the end of the rehearsal, not one fully assembled outfit had arrived.

De Mille, who was both choreographer and lead dancer of *Rodeo*, concentrated on her own role during the rehearsal. She leapt, turned, and capered, demonstrating not only the grace of a ballet star but the sure timing and wit of a gifted comic dancer. Her antics produced gratifying laughter from the rehearsal's few spectators. Exhausted after the session, de Mille went to her dressing room to rest. The 37-year-old dancer knew she needed her strength and energy for the evening to come, but she was too nervous to eat dinner.

*Rodeo*'s debut marked the most critical moment of de Mille's career to date: the unveiling of a work unlike anything previously seen onstage, a work she had created entirely on her own. Although her past performances had received critical acclaim, they had rarely made enough money to pay her living expenses. Her sympathetic mother, Anna de Mille, who knew she lived to dance and to compose new dances, had supplied her with financial and emotional support, and her sister, Margaret Fineman, often gave her clothes. But Agnes de Mille yearned for independence; if *Rodeo* succeeded, she would have it.

The dancers of the Ballet Russe de Monte Carlo, the company that would introduce *Rodeo* to the world, spent the hour before the performance calming their opening-night jitters with gos-

sip and jokes. As curtain time approached, they warmed up by stretching, supporting themselves on stepladders or on the back of the piano.

The warm-up on opening night was slow and careful; no one wanted to pull a muscle or strain a joint, especially just before a performance. Starting with pliés (knee bends) in all five classical ballet positions, the dancers moved to battements (leg lifts) and finally to relevés, rising up on their toes.

With muscles warm and limber, company members applied their stage makeup. Female dancers pinned their

*Partnered by Ballet Russe star Frederic Franklin, de Mille executes one of the high-stepping numbers she designed for* Rodeo. *The audience loved it.*

hair back and sprayed it in place until, as de Mille wrote in her autobiography *Dance to the Piper*, "they could be shaken like a rat in a terrier's mouth and not a strand would be loosened." The dancers smoothed pancake makeup from hairline to collarbone, then applied rouge, lipstick, eye shadow, false eyelashes, and mascara. Soon every face was perfect, ready to present to the audience.

De Mille shared a dressing room with one of the Ballet Russe's Russian dancers. As the two performers prepared for the stage, they were joined by the wife of Léonide Massine, the company's former choreographer. Watching de Mille dress and arrange her hair, Mrs. Massine asked if she was nervous. "I am," replied de Mille. "I am sick at my stomach."

"Good luck! Success!" said Massine.

De Mille turned to face her. "I hope we have success," the dancer said softly. "The success or failure of my life depends on the next half hour."

Several months earlier, the Ballet Russe had given de Mille a contract to choreograph a "cowboy" ballet, an assignment that represented a real honor to the aspiring American. At the time, the Ballet Russe was the most successful company in the world, lauded by critics and loved by audiences. Every dancer, it seemed, aspired to join the Ballet Russe; many non-Russian dancers even took Russian-sounding stage names to enhance their prestige. De Mille, as a guest choreographer and an American, was an outsider, but she would not let this intimidate her. Few

*Members of the internationally celebrated Ballet Russe company bid farewell to Chicago during the group's 1916 tour—its first—of the United States.*

American dance companies existed at the time, and de Mille wanted to use the opportunity to gain recognition for American art.

The ballet would have a simple story line, comic in places but also poignant. The plot focuses on Cowgirl, a young ranch woman who falls in love with the Champeen Roper. In order to be near him, she takes a job on his farm, where she dresses and acts like a man. But when everyone pairs off for the hoedown and The Champeen Roper continues to ignore her, Cowgirl realizes her plan has not worked; he sees her as just another farmhand, not as someone to escort to a dance.

Describing the role of Cowgirl, de Mille later said: "She's not really a tomboy. She's an adolescent who has outgrown her childhood and is not yet a woman.... It has to be [danced by] a very shy, passionate girl." Composer Aaron Copland's musical score for the ballet, particularly the lyrical "Saturday Night Waltz," underlines the young girl's conflicts and desires. The story has a happy ending: Cowgirl—performed by de Mille at the premiere—outdances everyone at the hoedown, winning the heart of The Champeen Roper.

When she first outlined the story to Aaron Copland, the composer had just looked at her in silence. "Well," said de Mille, "it isn't *Hamlet*." Copland roared with laughter, then agreed to write the ballet score. The composer, who later earned an international reputation for such works as *Appalachian Spring* and *The Tender Land*, was already well known. When he created the music for *Rodeo*, he drew on folk songs and square-dance tunes, adapting their melodies and rhythms to his own highly individual style. Working from Copland's score, de Mille set out to choreograph a ballet that would be equally remarkable.

Through her choreography, de Mille hoped to capture the distinctive verve and energy of the American West. After 14 years as a professional dancer, she wanted to test her ideas about a new art form that blended authentic folk themes with classical ballet as danced by the Ballet Russe. In 1938, de Mille had done a series of studies for Western-style dances performed by an all-female troupe. For *Rodeo*, she used some of the steps from her old ballet, styling them for a company that included male dancers and adding a plot. Then she had to teach the Russian company how to dance in an entirely new way.

Schooled in classical ballet, the dancers of the Ballet Russe had no idea how to walk like cowboys. As for their arms, de Mille observed in *Dance to the Piper*, "Alas, although big boys, they had been trained to move like wind-blown petals." She tried to explain the problem to the performers: "You have men's arms, they have striking power, they can control a heavy, moving rope or the brute furies of an 800-pound animal." But despite her words, she later recalled, "up came the delicate wrists and curled fingers of the 18th-century dandy."

All that had changed by the time *Rodeo* was ready to open. De Mille had taught the dancers how to pantomime the motions of horseback riding and cattle roping; now they could move as if propelled by an animal instead of by their own legs. Although another cowboy ballet, *Billy the Kid*, had been presented in New York two years earlier, de Mille's new ways of moving and dancing were unique. On opening night, she wondered if the audience would understand and enjoy her work.

Fifteen minutes before curtain time, the costumes were still not finished. The dancers waited nervously, some attired in their dressing gowns, some wearing parts of costumes in combination with their offstage clothing—a Western shirt over plain black practice tights; a pair of sun-faded pants under a dressing gown. As each shipment arrived by taxi, the dancers pounced on it, handing out the pieces to their respective wearers.

Out front, military uniforms mingled with fur coats and tuxedos as audience members took their seats in the glittering Metropolitan Opera House. Filled with the elite of New York society, the

*Male dancers perform* Billy the Kid, *a 1940 ballet choreographed by Eugene Loring. Like* Rodeo, Billy *had a western theme, but the two works were otherwise dissimilar.*

*Sol Hurok smiles as fans line up for one of his imported dance presentations. Until the 1940s, most ballet staged in America originated in Europe.*

theater was sold out. The crowd included the evening's manager, powerful impresario Sol Hurok, and the celebrated modern dancer Martha Graham, one of de Mille's closest friends. Also present were Theatre Guild executive Theresa Helburn, composer Richard Rodgers, and lyricist Oscar Hammerstein II. With a string of hits behind them—Rodgers was famed for *The Boys from Syracuse* and *Pal Joey*; Hammerstein, for *Desert Song* and *Show Boat*—the two showmen were working on a musical set in the Amer-

ican heartland. Intrigued by rumors about *Rodeo*, they had come to see de Mille's innovative "cowboy" choreography.

Meanwhile, tempers were flaring backstage; even the experienced dancers fidgeted tensely as the costumes slowly materialized at the stage door. At last, only minutes before curtain time, the last piece arrived. Miraculously, everything fit beautifully. The dancers went through their "good luck" rituals, crossing themselves, touching the wooden floor, spitting over one another's shoulders. "I'm going in," said conductor Franz Allers. He kissed de Mille and marched into the orchestra pit. Freddie Franklin, de Mille's partner, spat over her shoulder but didn't say a word.

"This was a terrible moment," recalled de Mille in *Dance to the Piper*, "but I had company." She looked at the "very great dancers" surrounding her, studying their muscled bodies and intense faces. "I knew I would never be alone again," she said. Then, as the dancers stood behind the gold curtains, "the large descending octaves sounded from the brass, sharp as sunlight on rocks. We flexed our insteps and breathed deep. The gold folds contracted. The music was suddenly clear under our feet. The naked, living dark yawned. 'This is it, kids,' said Freddie, without moving his lips."

De Mille exploded into action. The pent-up tension of waiting gave her extra energy, and she danced with furious concentration. Responding with roars of laughter at her subtly comic moves, the audience applauded her first exit. When one of the dancers missed an entrance, de Mille improvised for 64 bars of music to cover for him. No one in the audience seemed to notice the mistake.

Suddenly de Mille found it hard to breathe; her collar was too tight. Pausing for an instant at the rear of the stage, she whispered, "Freddie, I'm fainting. Loosen my collar." He replied, "No time, duckie. Here we go."

Franklin lifted, pushed, and carried her, his own feet pounding to the rhythms of Copland's music. The performance went quickly, allowing de Mille no time to reflect on it. She and her partner swung to center stage, then sailed to the footlights, separated, and danced the finale. The curtain dropped. As applause thundered, the curtain opened for de Mille and Franklin to take their bows.

Members of the Ballet Russe presented their American choreographer with a bouquet of corn tied with red, white, and blue ribbons. De Mille bowed again and again while the curtain opened and closed. After the eighth curtain call, she looked into the pit: The musicians were tapping their instruments and cheering, a rare but sure sign of approval. After 22 curtain calls, de Mille realized that *Rodeo* was a hit.

*New Englanders "promenade home" at a 1940 barn dance. In choreographing* Rodeo, *de Mille drew heavily on such typically American dance patterns.*

19

*Agnes de Mille, nine years old when she and her family left New York for California, already knew what she wanted to do with her life: dance.*

# T W O

# "I Never Sat Down"

Agnes George de Mille was born in New York City on September 18, 1905. Her father, William de Mille, was a successful playwright; his Broadway hits included *The Woman* and *The Warrens of Virginia*, a 1907 drama that gave future Hollywood goddess Mary Pickford her first role. Agnes's mother, Anna George de Mille, the daughter of prominent economist Henry George, actively crusaded for her father's tax-reform ideals. Anna de Mille's interests included not only economics but music, art, and literature.

Pretty and vivacious, Anna de Mille adored her dashing playwright husband. "That Father and Mother were in love I knew as I knew the woods were green and budding," their daughter recalled in her memoir of childhood, *Where the Wings Grow*. "They walked hand in hand; I remember . . . the look

he bent upon her, and the blue dazzle of her return gaze."

Agnes, who inherited her mother's outgoing nature, enjoyed being the center of attention, even as a toddler. One hot afternoon at Merriewold, the family's vacation residence in southwestern New York State, her mother gave her a bath, then rubbed olive oil onto her skin. "Go show Aunt Bettie," she told her daughter.

"Naked and glistening and smelling like a salad," little Agnes scampered out to see her aunt, then announced, "Now I'll show Father." Before her aunt could stop her, Agnes had marched over to the crowd of friends and relatives assembled at the family's tennis court. "Father stopped in mid-serve," she recalled later. "All heads turned. I continued my shining, silent advance." When her father told her to

*Anna George de Mille, dedicated tax reformer, daughter of Henry George, and mother of Agnes de Mille, sat for this oil portrait in her family's Manhattan apartment.*

her mother took her to see a performance by Adeline Genée, a celebrated Danish ballerina. Enchanted by the "dainty, doll-like, and impeccable" dancer, Agnes changed her plans: She would grow up to be a ballet star. Her parents declined to give her ballet lessons, but her mother encouraged her by playing the piano while her daughter improvised dances.

Agnes and her younger sister, Margaret, divided their early years between Manhattan ("head colds, walks in the park, curtailment of racing and screaming in the apartment") and Merriewold (being "free and wild for months and weeks and days"). But in 1914, the girls' peaceful routine changed suddenly. Dispirited by the resounding failure of his latest Broadway play, *After Five*, William de Mille accepted the invitation of his brother, Cecil, to join him in California. Anna de Mille liked the idea. The move, she said cheerfully, "would be so good for the children's colds."

In 1913, Cecil B. De Mille (unlike his older brother, Cecil used a capital *D* in spelling the family name) had founded one of the earliest movie studios. Motion pictures, then silent and flickering, seemed no more than a novelty to many people; Cecil B. De Mille was one of a handful of pioneers who recognized their true potential. Along with his partners, Jesse Lasky and Samuel Goldwyn, De Mille would become a giant in the industry, producing such spectacular hits as *Cleopatra* in 1934 and the Oscar-winning *Greatest Show on Earth* in 1952. In 1914, how-

go back to the house, Agnes turned and retraced her steps with great dignity. "That was my only lifelong exhibitionism," she wrote later. "It was, however, I believe, splendid; in the star position, uncurtailed, at the peak of the afternoon."

Anna and William de Mille often entertained prominent stage figures in their New York City apartment. Little Agnes, who gazed admiringly at the stylish actresses who came to call, intended to become one herself. Then, when she was about seven years old,

ever, De Mille was just beginning, and he needed help. Brother William, he pointed out, was "literate" and could write movie scripts.

The de Milles moved from New York City to Hollywood in 1914. Nine-year-old Agnes was delighted by the change. "I would have a horse and ride with the cowboys," she thought. "I would, please God, be allowed to act in the movies." After a week-long train trip across the country, the family arrived in California. They settled not on a ranch populated by horses and cowboys but in a simple house with a rose garden. Behind it, the Hollywood hills,

not yet covered with buildings and freeways, stood etched against the smog-free sky.

Agnes missed her home in the East. In California, "the summers were . . . brown earth, brown grass, bold sky," she wrote later. "My skin, my hair, my heart thirsted for green." Nevertheless, the western landscape made a deep impression on her. "It is no accident that California produced our greatest dancers," she observed in *Dance to the Piper*. "The Eastern states sit in their folded scenery, tamed and remembering, but in California the earth and sky clash, and space is dynamic. . . . The

*Trees surround the de Milles' vacation home in Merriewold, New York. To young Agnes, Merriewold summers meant "being free and wild for months and weeks and days."*

23

*Agnes's father, author William de Mille (left), and her uncle, movie mogul Cecil B. De Mille, confer outside William's Hollywood home in 1915.*

Douglas Fairbanks, Jr., and Joel McCrea, young men who would later become movie superstars. The Hollywood School offered dance classes, but Agnes was not allowed to enroll in them. Anna de Mille, who fervently believed in "self-expression," feared that lessons would spoil her daughter's "native gifts."

Agnes's mother held firm ideas about everything. She had "settled for herself the causes of war, of economic depression, of unequal distribution of wealth," said her daughter. She had also reached "definite conclusions on hats, dresses, interior decoration, manners, painting, music, plays, cooking, the rearing of children, and sex." Anna de Mille also believed in economy: She saved everything, from old letters to string to time. "Don't just sit there, dearie," she would command Agnes. "*Do* something!" As an adult, her daughter wrote, "To this hour I find it impossible to read a book before sundown unless it has some immediate connection with my work."

Although she insisted that her daughters make good use of their time, Anna de Mille raised no objections to Agnes's dancing: "Improvised dances," she asserted, were "cultural." As an adult, de Mille wondered what her mother really thought about her passion for dance. "What went on inside Mother's heart, while she watched me hop and race, I do not know," she wrote in *Dance to the Piper*. "I suspect she entertained some wild hopes. She admitted 20 years later that I was pretty

descending grassy slopes filled me with a passion to run, to roll in delirium, to wreck my body on the earth. Space means this to a dancer—or to a child!"

Agnes may have wanted to race through the hills, but her mother had other ideas. Two days after the family's arrival, she enrolled her older daughter in the Hollywood School for Girls, a private institution attended by several filmmakers' children. Despite the school's name, its pupils included

*Future film idol Douglas Fairbanks, Jr., de Mille's fellow student at the misnamed Hollywood School for Girls, models his costume for a class play.*

damn good, but naturally she said nothing of the sort then. She wanted me above all to be a fine, gentle, sweet-mannered, pure girl, and this was what I was being raised as against every inclination in my nature.''

That nature took permanent shape when she was about 12 years old. One unforgettable Saturday, her mother took her to a performance by Anna Pavlova, the era's best-known and most popular ballet star. Toast of her native Russia, the Incomparable Pavlova had been touring the United States since 1910, giving thousands of Americans their first view of classical ballet. From coast to coast, audiences thrilled to the tiny dancer's exquisite footwork and her romantic interpretations of such works as *The Sleeping Beauty*, performed to music by Russian composer Pyotr Tchaikovsky.

Almost four decades later, de Mille recalled her first sight of the celebrated ballerina: "Anna Pavlova! My life stops as I write that name. Across the daily preoccupation with lessons, lunch boxes, tooth brushings, and quarrelings with Margaret flashed this bright unworldly experience and burned in a single afternoon a path over which I could never retrace my steps.''

Her heart pounding, her throat burning, Agnes watched Pavlova's "beating, flashing, quivering legs" as she whirled across the stage. After the performance, Agnes was unable to speak. When she got home, she went up to her bedroom, shut the door, and began to dance. Clinging to the rail of her bed, she stood on tiptoe in her high-buttoned shoes and took as many steps as she could. Her toes throbbed, her knees ached, her legs shook; she cried. "Only by hurting my feet," she recalled, "could I ease the pain in my throat."

*Fifteen-year-old Agnes de Mille enjoys a fireside read. Because her mother encouraged "constructive activity," teenage Agnes experienced few such tranquil moments.*

Agnes soon translated her passion into action. Gathering her friends, she organized a dance pageant in her backyard. Her mother helped with costumes and music, and friends and neighbors applauded politely as the little girls twirled and pirouetted on the lawn. Nevertheless, Agnes's parents continued to refuse her pleas for dance lessons. Her mother still insisted that formal training would stifle her daughter's natural gifts, and her father wanted her to concentrate on her education.

Unlike his wife, William de Mille had little regard for dancing or female dancers, whom he considered neither "ladylike" nor "bright." One night Agnes discussed the issue with her father. Sitting in his study, after-dinner brandy in hand, he asked: "Do you honestly think, my daughter, that dancing has progressed since the time of the Greeks?"

"No," Agnes replied. "Do you think you write any better than Euripides [a great playwright of ancient Greece]?"

"No, my dear," he said. "But we have Euripides's plays. They have lasted. A dancer ceases to exist the minute she sits down."

Agnes, now 14, kept asking for lessons; her parents kept refusing. The situation, de Mille recalled later, "might have gone on this way for years if my sister's arches hadn't providentially fallen." The doctor consulted by the de Milles said Margaret's feet could be strengthened by ballet dancing. Because the sisters did everything to-

*Ballerina Anna Pavlova greets visitors in her backstage dressing room. When de Mille met her idol in 1919, the young dancer found herself speechless.*

*A costumed Agnes de Mille (top left) and her friends prepare for a dance pageant. The backyard ballet marked de Mille's debut as a choreographer.*

gether, ballet lessons for Margaret meant ballet lessons for Agnes. The girls enrolled in the Theodore Kosloff School of Imperial Russian Ballet.

Ten minutes after Agnes began her first lesson, she found herself aching, sweaty, and dizzy, and she asked permission to sit down. "You must never sit during practice," replied her teacher. "If you sit down you may not continue with class." De Mille, who would have preferred "a beating with whips" to ending her lesson, remained standing. Eventually, she recalled, she learned to combat faintness by relaxing with her head between her knees. She even learned how to bandage her toes "so that they would not bleed through the satin shoes." But, she added, "I never sat down." Despite her difficulties at ballet school, Agnes loved it. "Ah, but there was glory in that room," she wrote later.

Most of Kosloff's students attended classes and practice sessions every day, but the de Milles limited their daughters' classes to two each week, all they believed necessary for Margaret's therapy. Without a daily workout, Agnes knew she was doomed to mediocrity at best. She decided to practice at home, rising at 6:30 A.M. and going to school, doing her homework, and taking her piano and tennis lessons "at breakneck concentration" until 6:00 P.M.. Then she was free to practice in her mother's bathroom, which Anna de Mille had equipped with a small *barre*. (All dancers spend several hours a day at the barre, a wall-mounted wooden rail that supports dancers and helps them balance as they practice their steps.)

Without a teacher to guide her during these solitary workouts, Agnes inevitably made mistakes. "Every week," she recalled later, "I developed a new bad habit." Also working against her was her late start; most dancers start to learn their art by the age of nine. In addition, Agnes's parents, fearing that she would injure her health, forbade her to practice for more than 45 minutes a day.

Nevertheless, wrote de Mille in *Dance to the Piper*, "I learned the first and all-important dictate of ballet dancing—never to miss the daily practice, hell or high water, sickness or health, never to miss the barre practice; to miss meals, sleep, rehearsals, even, but not the practice, not for one day ever under any circumstances."

During Agnes's first year at the Kosloff School, Anna Pavlova made another appearance in Los Angeles. Given an afternoon off from school to watch the great dancer, Agnes awaited the day with both excitement and terror. Could her idol live up to the image she cherished in her memory? Or would Agnes, now much more knowledgeable about dance technique, find Pavlova a mere mortal? When the curtain rose, Agnes's doubts dissolved; Pavlova's dancing was as full of fire and magic as ever. "Oh, holy life! How could I have doubted her?" thought Agnes.

When the curtain fell, a family friend who knew Pavlova asked Agnes if she would like to meet her. Agnes was speechless. Her mother, who had accompanied her to the theater, spoke for her daughter. "She would. Yes," said Anna de Mille. Backstage, the friend pushed Agnes toward Pavlova. "This is Kosloff's best pupil," she said.

"Ah! Brava! Brava!" Pavlova replied. "Would you like some flowers?" The ballerina gathered carnations and cherry blossoms from the bouquets surrounding her. Then, recalled Agnes de Mille, "Anna Pavlova kissed me." The young dancer burst into happy tears.

De Mille kept the flowers for years. She kept studying, kept practicing, kept growing up and changing. She had been a pretty, slender little girl, but by the time she was 16, she wrote later, she found herself "suddenly imprisoned in someone else's body, heavy, deep-bosomed, large-hipped. . . . When I realized I was not going to be a beautiful woman, I gave up caring how I looked— or thought I did."

Margaret—"an extremely pretty girl, with a great sense of personal chic," said her sister—was besieged by eager suitors, but Agnes failed to charm the young men she met. "It was my practice to challenge boys immediately to a trial of strength on the tennis court, beat the hell out of them, and then dismiss them," she recalled later. "They were never asked back. Indeed, they seldom wanted to come."

Agnes insisted she did not mind being ignored by the boys. "I told myself with somber pride that when I was a great dancer with all the capitals of Europe at my feet, they would be very surprised indeed to remember they had passed me up," she noted in *Dance to the Piper*. Meanwhile, however, Agnes was growing discouraged with her

29

*The de Mille sisters arrange flowers in their Hollywood Boulevard home. Agnes (left) considered herself plain, but she described Margaret as "extremely pretty."*

lonely practice routine. As she danced alone, she could often hear her family and their guests—who included such exciting friends as comedian Charlie Chaplin, authors Michael Arlen and Somerset Maugham, and movie hero Douglas Fairbanks—laughing, singing, playing tennis, and watching movies. (By this time, Agnes's extremely successful screenwriter father had installed his family in a huge house, set in a five-acre garden on Hollywood Boulevard.) Convinced she was making no technical progress, she began to drcad her sessions at the barre. "By the time I got through high school," she wrote later, "dancing meant exhaustion and little else."

The summer after she graduated from high school, Agnes de Mille made a decision. One morning, she approached her father, who was shaving, and said, "Pop, I've decided to give up dancing and go to college." William de Mille kept his eyes on the mirror. "I'm glad you have, my dear," he replied calmly. "I don't think you would have been happy." One week later, Agnes de Mille entered the University of California at Los Angeles. For the first time since the age of 13, she stopped practicing at the barre every day.

De Mille lived at home during her four years of college, driving to and from the campus in her father's battered old Buick. Applying the furious concentration she had once devoted to dancing, she threw herself into her studies. "I did nothing but work," she recalled. As a freshman, de Mille attended no football games, no dances, no sorority teas. And, she added, "I did not have one date." Encouraged by her teachers' praise, she developed a new interest: writing. Although she found it almost as much hard work as dancing, writing offered one luxury. "One could do it," she noted, "sitting down."

But de Mille's passion for dancing refused to disappear. In her sophomore year at college, she performed at a school benefit show; the next year, she presented a skit on the history of jazz

*Garbed as exotic East Indian dancers, de Mille (left) and a friend await the start of a ballet concert on the University of California campus.*

dancing. Inevitably, she slipped back into her old practice routines, working out after she had finished studying and the rest of the household had retired. De Mille danced as quietly as she could, but one night her practice routine was suddenly interrupted. Emerging from his study with his pipe in one hand and a book in the other, William de Mille contemplated his dancing daughter, her face "blanched and wet with weariness." He shook his head. "All this education," he said, "and I'm still just the father of a circus."

*De Mille performs one of her most popular works:* Ballet Class, *a comic "character sketch" in which she portrayed a young dancer afflicted with stage fright.*

# THREE

# Tryouts

Joking about her years in college, de Mille claimed they had taught her three important things: "To use a library, to memorize quickly and visually, [and] to drop asleep at any time, given a horizontal surface and 15 minutes." In fact, however, she had excelled at the University of California, and she graduated *cum laude* (with honor).

By the time she earned her degree, de Mille had decided on her "misty future": She would become a professional dancer. But before she could tell her parents about her plan, they told her about their own. After 23 years of marriage, Anna and William de Mille intended to divorce. "Suddenly," wrote their shocked daughter, "the future was in my face." Acceding to Anna de Mille's wishes, Agnes and her sister accompanied her to Europe immediately. A summer abroad, thought

Agnes, might help soothe her mother's anguish at learning that her husband wanted to marry a younger woman.

To demonstrate support for her mother, Agnes de Mille severed her ties to her beloved father, a move that pained her deeply. It also deprived her of the benefit of her father's theatrical experience and contacts, assets that might have smoothed her path toward success.

When the three de Mille women returned to the United States late in 1927, they settled in New York, a city bursting with excitement and energy. On Broadway, "the Great White Way," stars were born overnight and vanished just as quickly. Prohibition had outlawed the sale of alcohol, but people who wanted to drink gathered at speakeasies (illegal bars) or bought their supplies from the gangsters known as

33

*Even in the rain, New York City's Times Square gleams seductively. Determined to succeed as a dancer, de Mille hit the "Great White Way" in 1927.*

bootleggers. Jazz clubs flourished in Harlem, and flappers—young women with bobbed hair and shockingly short skirts—smoked cigarettes, wore lipstick, and danced the Charleston. The Roaring Twenties were in full flower.

"These were the days," de Mille later recalled, "of speakeasy money on Broadway . . . of dancers hired on the sheen of the stocking and the wink of their agent . . . of the sexy rhinestone, the zip, the boom, the guts, the speed, the hot-diggety dirt. This was the profession of my choosing, this corrupt carnival."

Half-serious, she considered her qualifications: She could speak impeccable English; she could use a library; she knew what she considered beautiful. On the other hand, she had never bought so much as a hat without her mother's advice, never looked for a job, never even been kissed. She was also "stiff in the joints, overweight and underpracticed." Thus equipped, she faced a theater "which for sheer toughness and vulgarity had few counterparts in the history of the stage." Had she known what lay ahead of her, she commented in *Dance to the Piper*, she would "not have had the courage to go on."

Anna de Mille, who had received a large financial settlement from her ex-husband, rented an expensive apartment and insisted that her daughters move in with her. She devoted herself to helping Agnes pursue success as a dancer, partially as a way of forgetting her own unhappiness. "Her pride had been broken. She was a desperate woman," observed her daughter. "She married me and as a wedding gift she gave me my career."

Anna de Mille's own words, quoted in her daughter's diary, make her feelings clear: "I who have always been known as the daughter of my father, and the wife of my husband, pray that someday I will be known as the mother of my daughter."

Hoping to find work on Broadway, de Mille made the rounds of the New York theatrical producers and agents. Most of them agreed to see her only because she was the daughter and niece of Hollywood's celebrated de Mille brothers. When the Broadway moguls realized she had neither experience nor backing from her famous relatives, they wished her luck and sent her on her way.

De Mille auditioned whenever she heard about a new show, but although she tried and tried, she got no parts. One well-meaning friend suggested a formula for success: First, de Mille should change her name to something more theatrical than plain "Agnes"; next, she should dye her hair a brilliant shade of red, which would better reflect

the spotlight. While she was at it, said de Mille's friend, she should get her teeth straightened and her nose shortened. "All these suggestions," de Mille recalled, "I resisted with unexpected stubbornness. I was determined to survive, if at all, as me."

De Mille kept auditioning. Before long, she said, she had "danced before every known manager and agent in New York." As the winter wore on and she had still received no job offers, her normally buoyant spirits began to flag. Gazing at the rain one day, she "won-

*A pair of flappers demonstrate the latest steps. The "Jazz Babies" of the Roaring Twenties shocked their elders by wearing rolled stockings and short skirts.*

*Anna de Mille—seen here flanked by her daughters Margaret (left) and Agnes in 1928—devoted herself to helping Agnes achieve success as a dancer.*

dered if a dear little wet coffin would not be most comforting." Fortunately, her mother's support and enthusiasm tempered her despair, and a trip to the Southwest lifted her spirits.

Anna de Mille needed to appear in a California court to finalize her divorce, and she decided to take her daughter along. On the way to the West Coast, the women stopped in Santa Fe, New Mexico, to visit writer Mary Austin, an old family friend. Famed for its scenic beauty and clear air, Santa Fe was home to many painters and writers. There, at Austin's urging, de Mille gave a dance concert.

The women rented a hall, ordered tickets, hired a pianist, and paid for a notice in the local newspaper. At the time, this was the standard way to stage a dance concert: Dancers advanced the rent for concert halls out of their own pockets, or in de Mille's case, out of her mother's. Only if the proceeds from ticket sales met or exceeded expenses would the dancer break even or make a profit. Otherwise, the dancer lost money. Concert dancing was an expensive proposition.

Just before the concert, Austin rushed up to de Mille and her mother. "We've done it! We've done it!" she exclaimed. "We're clear! Three hundred and sixty-four dollars in cold cash. The expenses are paid!" The women gave the rest of the tickets away, most of them to Austin's American Indian friends. Austin had seen them perform their dances; now she wanted them to see an example of contemporary ballet.

Members of the local artist's colony loved de Mille's work. Comparing her to America's most famous dancer, they hailed her as "the next Isadora Duncan." But the American Indians in the audience reacted differently. After the concert, Austin explained the Indians' attitude. In their culture, she told de Mille, the earth is the source of all strength, and dancing on it affirms the bond between worshipers and their god. Because dance is a mystical ritual through which both the dancer and the god receive strength, de Mille's dancing *en pointe*—on the tips of her toes— struck the Indians as absurd.

Austin advised de Mille to learn from Native American culture regarding the spiritual power of dance. De Mille, she said, should draw her energy as a dancer

*Costumed—more or less—as an American Indian, Jacques Cartier performs a "war dance." De Mille's 1928 concert with Cartier produced critical praise but no money.*

from her own native roots. "You must let the rhythm of the American earth come through what you do," she said. De Mille never forgot Austin's words. In later years, as she sought to create a uniquely American dance form, she came to live by them.

When she returned to New York, de Mille continued to audition for dance roles. The following winter, in 1928, she finally won the opportunity to appear in a dance recital. She would share the expenses and receive second billing to Jacques Cartier, a moderately successful American dancer. For her part of the program, de Mille decided to dance a series of what she called "character sketches." In *Ballet Class*, based on a painting by 19th-century French artist Edgar Degas, she impersonated a frightened young dance student. In *'49*, she became a "covered-wagon girl" in the 1849 California gold rush. This sketch, de Mille noted later, "was, to my knowledge, the first use of American folk material on the concert stage."

After a month of rehearsals, the recital opened to a packed house. Handed a telegram from her father just before curtain time, de Mille was deeply touched to read: WELCOME, MY DAUGHTER, INTO THE PROFESSION. *Stage Fright*, de Mille's first number, produced an enormous round of applause and—to the dancer's amazement—cheers, whistles, and loud laughter. "I found I was a comedian," she wrote later. "It seems I was very funny, I who always wanted to die for beauty." Delighted, she went on to perform *'49*, which the audience greeted with even greater enthusiasm.

De Mille's dancing also impressed *New York Times* dance critic John Martin. Reviewing the recital the following day, he wrote: "Here is undoubtedly one of the brightest stars now rising above our native horizon."

Despite critical enthusiasm and

three nights of sellout crowds, Cartier's manager told de Mille that the show had made no money. When she asked him for an accounting, he presented her with a handful of unpaid bills and disappeared. De Mille realized she had made a serious financial mistake by dancing without a contract. But she had no regrets. The recital, she thought, had been "an auspicious start."

A few months later, de Mille learned that a pair of prestigious British producers had arrived in New York to cast dancers for their new review. De Mille arranged for an audition and, full of high hopes, performed four of her latest character sketches. The producers thanked her politely. Her work was good, they said, but it was strictly concert-hall material. In their opinion, she would never find a place in the theater.

*Chorus-line dancers rehearse for a Broadway musical. Although New York City abounded with song-and-dance shows in the 1920s, de Mille searched for a job in vain.*

"This verdict," de Mille noted grimly, "had come from the top men of the trade." When she got home, her mother took her weeping daughter in her arms. "My father used to say that a way would become apparent as we go along," Anna de Mille said gently. "In the end a door always opens."

Strengthened by her mother's boundless faith and her own determination, de Mille kept on. Not long after her crushing rejection by the British producers, she was offered a spot as guest soloist on a national ballet tour. Managing the tour was Adolph Bolm, a former Ballet Russe star who had often partnered Anna Pavlova. Clearly "second-string," the tour played to nearly empty theaters in the South and Midwest. But Bolm thrilled de Mille with tales about the incomparable Pavlova and the triumphs he had once shared with her.

Bolm reminisced about performing in Paris, where audience members had stormed over the footlights and carried him to his dressing room on their shoulders. He told de Mille about the sumptuous banquets that admirers gave dancers in the early 20th century and about touring with Pavlova in Scandinavia, where adoring fans showered them with roses in midwinter. Thinking about Pavlova, Bolm would sigh. "How he cherished her!" thought de Mille, who well understood his feelings.

When the tour ended, de Mille found herself a new assignment: choreographing and dancing in *The Black Crook*, a play scheduled to open in Hoboken, New Jersey. The engagement marked the first time de Mille had ever arranged dances for a group. Although she thoroughly enjoyed working on *The Black Crook*, chaos reigned over rehearsals and continued through opening night.

*Adolph Bolm demonstrates the style that made him a Ballet Russe star in the early 1900s. By the time he met de Mille, Bolm's dancing days were over.*

Because the play was unusually long—it ran for five and one-half hours—most of the audience, including the New York drama critics, left before it was over. One reviewer, however, *New York Times* dance critic John Martin, stayed to the end. The following Sunday, he wrote a long, highly favorable review in the *Times*, but, de Mille noted sadly, "no agent or manager ever read a dance critic, so it didn't help commercially." Nevertheless, theatergoers flocked to the play.

Soon after opening night, de Mille's partner accidentally kicked her in the face, breaking her nose. "The sound, a kind of wet scrunch, carried to the back of the theater," she reported, "but, I am proud to say, neither of us missed a step." The show continued to provide de Mille with problems. New Yorkers, she complained, came to New Jersey to drink beer spiked with rubbing alcohol (Prohibition was still in force) and "arrived late at the theater, very high, not to say a little crazy." To show their approval of the play, they bombarded the stage with everything from peanuts to programs. After three months of this, de Mille quit the show to try her luck elsewhere.

For what she called "a period that seemed endless," de Mille did her best to make herself known in the theater. She danced in a Baltimore movie theater, a Broadway chorus line, a shabby nightclub, and a short movie feature. "All I balked at," she recalled later, "was jigging on the sidewalk with a tambourine." Finally, she decided to visit her old home, Hollywood, then the center of the motion-picture world.

Arriving in California with her mother, de Mille hired a theater and announced a dance recital. The night of the performance found many of the film community's brightest lights at the Music Box Theatre; de Mille's old friends, teachers, and schoolmates came, as did many of her parents' friends. Among the audience members were William de Mille and his new wife. Breaking her long silence, his daughter had telephoned him and invited him to the recital. Her mother, still brokenhearted over the divorce, refused to give her former husband so much as a glance.

The audience, de Mille recalled, "behaved splendidly," laughing, cheering, and applauding. The next day, she met with her father at his office. When she walked in, he just looked at her. Then he spread his arms and his daughter rushed into them. Agnes, who had "been caught between two heartbreaks," wept with joy.

Impressed with his niece's recital, Cecil B. De Mille offered to bankroll her in a nationwide tour, complete with a large dance company, a manager, and a press agent. Could she be ready, he asked, in two months? Agnes, who had spent three years creating "six good dances," told her uncle it would take her at least two years to prepare for such a mammoth undertaking. Shocked by her response, Cecil told her that stars were "made of brilliant showmanship, not time." Agnes de Mille repeated that two months was out of the question. Cecil De Mille lost interest. "He never made the offer again," reported the dancer.

During her travels with Bolm's troupe, de Mille had learned the value of privacy, of having a room to herself at the end of the day. When she returned to New York from Hollywood, she resolved to make a few changes in her life. She moved out of her mother's apartment and into her own flat, where she spent the next four years. She remained within walking distance of her mother's apartment, so she could drop by for dinner or a chat at any time.

Free to do as she pleased, de Mille spent much of her time in her dance tunic, sketching out and practicing new movements. During these years, scores of dedicated, innovative dancers worked in New York; every Sunday, several of them gave recitals. Like every other dancer in town, de Mille spent her Sundays dashing from one recital to another. After she had attended several performances by Martha Graham, whose work she admired and respected most of all, de Mille met and became good friends with her.

*Martha Graham performs* Letter to the World, *a ballet based on the poems of Emily Dickinson. "Each time I saw her," wrote de Mille of her friend Graham, "I saw more."*

Graham, who had already earned public recognition, often visited de Mille at her hotel, where the pair spent endless hours discussing their work. De Mille wanted to study with her friend, but Graham considered their styles too dissimilar for such an arrangement to work. While she created free-form works that ignored established rules of dance, de Mille worked in a more traditional ballet style, making her own innovations. Nonetheless, de Mille valued the guidance of her friend, now regarded as one of the greatest dancers of the 20th century.

When de Mille questioned her own ability, gloomily wondering if she would ever succeed in staging her own dances, Graham offered words of comfort and support. "We all go through this," she said one day. "You are being tempered. You are a sword in the fire. Be glad. There is achievement ahead."

Alone in her room at the hotel, de Mille continued to work on her own dances. Although she still received an

*De Mille tries an outdoor rehearsal for her popular* Harvest Reel, *a dramatic solo piece in which she always wore a black wool dress.*

allowance from her father, it was not enough to pay for a self-sponsored recital. She yearned to go to Europe, where concert expenses were much lower, but even that was beyond her means. Then, in 1932, Bernard Fineman, the M-G-M executive her sister had married two years earlier, offered her a loan. Gratefully accepting it, the 27-year-old dancer set sail for France, accompanied by her mother.

De Mille appeared in two recitals in Paris, followed by one in Brussels, Belgium, but none fulfilled her high hopes. A series of misunderstandings, combined with an unscrupulous theatrical agent, resulted in almost no advance publicity in Paris. Because few Parisians knew of de Mille's appearance, the recital hall was only half filled, although those who attended applauded loudly.

At first, the situation in Brussels proved even more distressing. This time the audience made no response to the performance. "I went through every dance as programmed," de Mille wrote later. "Not a laugh. Not a sound. It was like a two-hour-long audition before hostile agents." Leaving the stage in "tears of vexation and shame," she met the theater manager, who greeted her with a broad smile. "Mademoiselle, you are a success," he told the surprised dancer. "I congratulate you."

The manager explained that the audience's silent response was typical in Belgium. If theatergoers disliked a show, he said, they simply walked out. Because no one, including the reviewers, had departed, he counted de Mille's

On Wednesdays
October 31st, November 7th
and November 14th
at 8.45 p.m.

THE
MERCURY
THEATRE
*presents*

AGNES de MILLE
in
*Three Dance Recitals*

At the Piano :
NORMAN FRANKLIN
& CHARLES LYNCH

Prices (including tax) : 7/6, 5/-, 3/6, 2/6
Two lines, PARK 1000, PARK 7233

*A London handbill advertises three 1934 de Mille performances. As the American dancer had hoped, the British capital responded to her work with "kindness."*

performance a triumph. Confirming his prediction, the next morning's reviews contained warm praise for the American dancer.

Mother and daughter left Brussels for London, site of the dancer's next recital. They would find the British capital shrouded in a steady gray drizzle. But here the sun would finally begin to shine on de Mille's career. "London," she said later, "was kind to us."

*At 27, de Mille found herself in the midst of London's social whirl,
entertained by society matrons, composers, film stars, and playwrights.*

# FOUR

# London Lessons

When the de Mille women arrived in England, actor Romney Brent, an old friend of the family's, took them under his wing. Popular with both London's high society and its theatrical world, Brent took de Mille to teas and parties with such contemporary stars as actor/playwright/composer Noël Coward, film star Raymond Massey, actress Dame May Whitty, and dance director Marie Rambert. Each time he presented de Mille to his friends, Brent announced, "This is the greatest pantomimic artist in the world!" His enthusiasm appeared to be contagious: When de Mille staged a dance recital at London's Arts Theatre Club, every seat was occupied.

The concert not only broke even financially but also provided de Mille with cheers from the audience, generous reviews from the critics, and an invitation from Marie Rambert. A celebrated ballet director, Rambert operated the small but influential dance company and school known as the Ballet Club. When she asked de Mille to give a series of concerts at her theater and to study dance between shows, the young American accepted quickly.

In the spring of 1933, Anna de Mille returned to New York, leaving her daughter completely on her own for the first time in her life. Agnes settled into a room at the English-Speaking Union, a residence in the Mayfair district of London, and began to work with Rambert.

Classes at the Ballet Club proved both exciting and unpredictable. Rambert had been known to throw chairs, roll on the floor, and scream when her pupils' performances failed to please her. But despite her temperament, she

*The moment she arrived at London's Victoria Station (above), de Mille fell in love with England. The feeling was mutual: "Thank you, America, for de Mille," wrote one reviewer.*

earned deep respect as a teacher and choreographer, and she attracted talented and loyal students. Among them were two future giants of the dance world: Antony Tudor, soon to become a ground-breaking choreographer with America's Ballet Theatre, and Hugh Laing, later celebrated as a brilliant dance soloist.

Tudor and Laing, who shared a London apartment, made a vivid impression on de Mille. She later recalled Laing as "the most beautiful young man I ever saw in my life." Sometimes, she said, "he was bonny and merry," but on bad days, "he was a tiger." She described Tudor as "fine-boned, quiet and thoughtful with characteristically wicked British humor." Awed by his talent, she called him "one of the natural forces of our time."

Tudor and Laing quickly adopted de

Mille as their protégée and close friend. ("I am not alone in this alien land," she remembered thinking. "I have folks.") The three dancers worked together at the Ballet Club, practiced at the men's apartment, and spent hours walking along the Thames River, discussing dance and choreography. Tudor stage-managed de Mille's dance concerts, and Laing became her steady dance partner.

During her first year in London, de Mille danced regularly, drawing consistently favorable remarks in the press. Her Degas-inspired character sketches, said one critic, were "tragic and tender and beautiful"; another reviewer closed his comments by saying, "Thank you, America, for de Mille." The London *Times* called her "an artist of an exceptional order" with "a touch of comic genius."

De Mille's growing reputation led to an interview with theatrical producer Charles Cochran and her first secure job in England. Planning a new musical, *Nymph Errant*, Cochran was in the market for a talented choreographer. He hired de Mille to create dances for the show, which would feature words and music by the celebrated American composer Cole Porter. Heading the cast was Gertrude Lawrence, the British musical-comedy queen who later starred in the original Broadway production of *The King and I*. "This time," de Mille observed happily, "I was joining the Big League."

In October 1933, *Nymph Errant* opened to rave notices. De Mille's choreography stopped the show and re-

ceived critical acclaim. But despite the sellout crowds, de Mille received no royalties: Her contract assured her only a modest weekly fee during the rehearsals of the show. Even for a newcomer, it was a bad contract, but de Mille had been so pleased to get the job that she had signed it without argument.

She continued to give recitals, some of which actually paid for themselves. Particularly popular with British audiences were the de Mille dances that reflected her American roots. *'49*, her sketch about the 1849 California gold rush, and her New York–accented *Blues* and *Strip Tease* always produced cheers. These concerts, while highly praised and well attended—by her old

*Dancer Hugh Laing, described by de Mille as the "most beautiful young man I ever saw," became her regular ballet partner in England.*

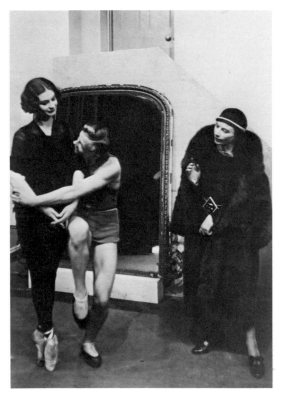

*Ballet director Marie Rambert instructs dancers at her London school. Impressed with de Mille's dancing, Rambert invited the young American to join her Ballet Club.*

and moved to an attic room whose only warmth came from a coin-operated heater. "For the first time in my life," she said later, "I knew real cold." In early 1934, she faced the fact that, for the moment, further recitals were financially out of the question. "If only I could get a job!" she wrote to her mother. (British law prohibited American citizens from working in England.) But de Mille remained hopeful. "There will be an American job one day, and I will take it," she told her mother. "If only Uncle Ce would offer me something!"

Two months later, her wish came true: "Uncle Ce"—Hollywood mogul Cecil B. De Mille—cabled his niece, asking her to choreograph and appear in the dance sequences of his next movie. Entitled *Cleopatra*, the film would be a lavish epic about the ancient Egyptian queen and her times. De Mille would receive $250 per week. "I flew; I raced; I leaped to accept," she recalled.

De Mille's friends assembled to wish her luck. "I'm off to dance with a crocodile," she shouted, referring to her Uncle Cecil's "extraordinary fancies." But her high spirits faltered when she reached New York and read the *Cleopatra* script. It called for her to wear a skimpy "showgirl" costume and dance on the back of a live bull. De Mille wondered what she had gotten herself into. She boarded the train for Hollywood, she wrote later, with "great eagerness but a certain apprehension."

Cecil B. De Mille, recalled his niece, "had wonderful charm." But, she

schoolmate Douglas Fairbanks, Jr., and Gertrude Lawrence, among others— wiped out what little money de Mille had saved from her *Nymph Errant* salary. Her father, hard hit by the Great Depression of the 1930s, was no longer able to maintain her allowance; her mother's income had also been sharply reduced. "I was broke," observed de Mille. "The picnic was over. Now I faced life like other dancers."

De Mille gave up her comfortable quarters at the English-Speaking Union

added, "he always got his way." Nobody ever disagreed with "the Chief" or refused his orders. He knew what he wanted. And what he wanted for his new film was sexy, scantily clad women wriggling seductively to the sensuous music of the Middle East.

Agnes de Mille knew what *she* wanted, too. "I would not like to do a dance of a man whipping half-naked girls dressed as leopards," she told her uncle firmly. "I should so love to do something mysterious, beautiful, new. Beautiful movement," she added, "not belly grinds and bumps." Cecil De Mille "bit his lip and shook his head," recalled his niece, but he grudgingly agreed to let her develop the dances in her own way.

Four weeks of hard work later, de Mille was ready to show her uncle one of the new dance sequences. She spent two painful hours with the studio's costume and makeup staff before the performance. Following the Chief's orders, cosmeticians plucked the dancer's eyebrows, covered her hair with black grease, remodeled her mouth with heavy lipstick, and coated her body with brown dye. Her costume—a gauzy skirt attached to a jeweled belt and a filmy top held in place by a wide metallic collar—was anchored to her skin with surgical tape. Intent on doing the job right, technicians removed and repositioned the outfit three times; "gouts of blood," recalled the dancer, "sprang out all over my back and shoul-

*In* Nymph Errant's *comic "Solomon" scene, a sultan laments having too many wives. Choreographed by de Mille, the 1933 London musical starred British actress Gertrude Lawrence.*

*After a London visit that included several de Mille dance recitals, Hollywood actor Douglas Fairbanks, Jr., heads home from Manhattan's Grand Central Station.*

ders." The crew offered sympathy. "Think of me as a doctor," said one dresser. "This has got to be done. I'm the best at it. And there's no time."

"Hurry up. Send her down," De Mille barked through the studio intercom. "Breathing prayers," Agnes de Mille approached the set, a model of Cleopatra's palace. As her uncle peered down from a towering black marble throne, she began to dance. The jeweled collar broke twice, and de Mille stopped for repairs. On the third try, she completed the piece, mounted the steps to her uncle's marble throne, and dropped a flower at his feet.

Silence blanketed the set. Not one of the 50 spectators—cast, staff, and technicians—moved. Then Cecil B. De Mille shook his head. "This has nothing," he said slowly. "It may be authentic, but it has no excitement, no thrill, no suspense, no sex."

"It had beauty," murmured the costume designer.

"What happened to the bull?" the producer demanded. He descended the marble steps, walked away, then turned to his regular choreographer. "Take this number and make something out of it we can photograph!" he commanded, and left the set.

The bull kept its role in *Cleopatra*, but de Mille did not. Five minutes after her uncle's stormy exit, she was off the studio payroll; the finished version of *Cleopatra* contained none of her work. Cecil B. De Mille was careful to protect his niece's reputation, citing "artistic differences" as the reason for her departure. Still, no one in the film industry would hire a choreographer who could not work successfully with the most powerful man in Hollywood, let alone with her own uncle.

The *Cleopatra* fiasco sparked long-simmering family tension and ended de Mille's hopes of a Hollywood career. It also left her "badly mauled" emotionally. "It was the stunning fact," she wrote in her memoir *Speak to Me, Dance with Me*, "that my family, my powerful world-renowned family, had offered practical help and then thrown me away as trash." De Mille had hoped

*Cecil B. De Mille (seated at right) films a scene from* Cleopatra. *Despite scathing reviews, the mammoth 1934 movie earned box-office millions.*

her father would stick up for her, but he only smiled wryly when she told him the story. "You wished to be a professional," he said. "[Cecil] treated you like one. Now you know."

De Mille spent the next few months studying and practicing in London, then returned to New York to arrange for a concert. But despite the help of her mother and a crowd of supportive friends, despite intensive efforts, rehearsals, and preparations, the performance received cruel reviews in the city's newspapers. John Martin of the *Times,* who had praised de Mille's work in the past, now asserted that she had stayed away from her roots too long and had failed to keep up with new currents in American dance.

Disappointed but not defeated, de Mille once again headed for California. There she received a novel proposal: The management of the Hollywood Bowl—a gigantic open-air theater seating 20,000 people—asked her to stage a dance spectacular for a fee of $2,000. De Mille had never had so much money to spend in her life, but with it she would have to pay and costume a troupe of 60 dancers. This expensive venture proved even more disastrous than the New York concert. "We danced our damnedest," recalled de Mille, but to no avail. The amphitheater's immense size overwhelmed the performers, and the lighting system failed to work properly, leaving the audience peering restlessly at an almost-dark stage. Brutal reviews appeared the next day: DE MILLE GIRL FAILS, read one newspaper headline.

De Mille spent the next few months at her sister's house, giving lessons, taking lessons, and "waiting for something or other to happen." At last, in the fall of 1935, something did happen: Director George Cukor asked de Mille to choreograph the dances for a major new film version of Shakespeare's *Romeo and Juliet.* Featuring top Hollywood stars Norma Shearer and Leslie Howard, the movie would also include hundreds of lesser actors and dozens of dancers. "I accepted," recalled de Mille, "with unbusinesslike alacrity [speed]."

Following Cukor's orders, de Mille designed three elaborate dance numbers, complete with a choir of little boys carrying golden apple trees and singing a medieval folk song. Ready on schedule—four months later—de Mille watched in shock as the cameramen photographed her dances. Each scene turned into a series of close-up shots of Shearer and Howard, with the dancers visible only as fleeting background images. When she saw the final print of

*Holding her Uncle Cecil's arm, de Mille checks the* Cleopatra *set. At right is the producer-director's actress daughter Katherine, costumed for her role in a Mae West film.*

the film, de Mille recalled later, she "went outside the projection room and lay down in the grass and was very, very sick."

De Mille's dances had cost not only thousands of hours of effort but more than $100,000, a tremendous sum in 1935. But the money, she insisted, had not been wasted: "The dances were *good*." The smash success of *Romeo and Juliet* also offered some consolation; "It is still playing in Nicaragua," de Mille dryly remarked many years later.

Because of her association with the popular *Romeo and Juliet*, de Mille soon received another assignment: choreographing a Broadway-bound musical entitled *Hooray for What*. Connected with the 1937 project were playwrights Howard Lindsay and Russel Crouse, later responsible for *The Sound of Music*; Harold Arlen and E. Y. Harburg, who would go on to write the songs for *The Wizard of Oz*; and Vincente Minnelli, future Oscar-winning director of *Gigi* (and father of entertainer Liza Minnelli). With such a "notable group of names," observed de Mille, "one would think they might insure a high degree of professionalism. It turned out not."

*Hooray* gave de Mille nothing but trouble from the start. The show's backers, whom she defined as "faded, jaded, raddled with drink, hawk-eyed, hard-mouthed, and insolent," forced her to hire female dancers of their own choice. "I had to take them," she recalled, "and I couldn't fire them, not if they fell down dead drunk at my feet,

*As star Norma Shearer watches intently, choreographer de Mille demonstrates a step she has designed for the 1936 film version of Shakespeare's* Romeo and Juliet.

*Standing alone (at left),* Romeo and Juliet *choreographer Agnes de Mille watches Norma Shearer (center) dance amid a chorus of young dancers bearing golden apple trees.*

not if they were three hours late." The business managers insisted on "tricky" costumes—one consisted mainly of rubber wire and a gas mask—that severely hampered the dancers' movements. The director ordered sets changed without informing the choreographer.

To complete the dismal picture, de Mille recalled, everybody in the company hated everyone else, "screaming and reviling one another across the theater." When leading lady Hannah Williams burst into tears one day, her husband, heavyweight champion Jack Dempsey, prowled the aisles, "wanting to poke someone but not rightly knowing whom," said de Mille. Along with half the company, de Mille was fired from the show before it opened. She responded with "something terse and four-lettered" and departed with relief.

And that, she recalled ironically, was "what the musical theater was like, full of glamour."

Planning to live on the money she had saved from *Romeo and Juliet* and *Hooray for What*, de Mille hastened back to London. There, she moved into an empty town house offered by a friend, rounded up 12 young dancers, and began to train them. Six months later, she recalled in *Dance to the Piper*, "we had the makings of a suite of American dances, one of which was called *Rodeo*." While she was developing these works, unveiled in April 1938, de Mille gave a series of solo concerts with Hugh Laing. The press, she noted with pride, "was uniformly good."

By September 1938, the dark shadow of World War II (which would begin the following year) already loomed over England. Preparing itself for the conflict, the British government sent thousands of noncitizens, de Mille among them, back to their own countries. As she packed her belongings, the 33-year-old dancer considered her progress over the past few years: "I had developed a passable ballet technique and I had learned to run off concerts without accident or collapse," she noted. "I had learned to organize and execute projects without family participation."

*Irate when the* Hooray for What *producers insulted his wife, heavyweight champion Jack Dempsey (above) strode into the theater "wanting to poke someone," reported de Mille.*

Most important, she said, "I had learned at last to live on my own strength." Knowing she would need that strength, she sailed for home.

*Returning to the United States just before the start of World War II, 33-year-old de Mille moved into a small apartment in New York City's Greenwich Village.*

# FIVE

# Success at Last

When de Mille returned to New York in the fall of 1938, she moved into a two-room studio in Greenwich Village. Her mother had urged her to come and live in the large apartment she shared with Margaret, now divorced, but de Mille preferred solitude. "I had determined that the purpose of my life was to make up dances," she recalled. "I wanted them to be good dances. I thought it wise to stick it out ... alone."

For the next four years, de Mille supported herself on $20 per week, money she earned teaching dance at the Young Men's Hebrew Association. Because she could not afford rental fees for concert halls, she temporarily stopped giving recitals, but she continued to practice. In 1940 she organized a group of equally impoverished choreographers; they split the cost—$5 per week—of a rehearsal studio and supplied each other with professional advice, local gossip, and much-needed emotional support.

"My life was really quite cozy, and it certainly was private," de Mille recalled in her autobiography. "There were only two unbearable hours between dinner and bed, but I'd learned a number of dodges for getting through these without facing up to my situation. This I was aware of dimly always, whether I wished to be or not. . . . The condition was close and never departing, like a head cold. I think the name of the state is despair, but I never dignified it by any such resounding title; I just went along grumbling."

By the time she was 36, de Mille had danced in five different countries, given recitals in concert halls and movie theaters, performed at parties and charitable events. She had choreographed dances on stage and in Hollywood, designed and made costumes, and toured with a ballet troupe. She had, as she put it, done "anything and everything to get a stage under my feet and an audience seated and watching." But none of it, she noted sadly, had led to anything else.

Beginning to wonder if her efforts would ever bear fruit, de Mille seriously considered giving up her career and applying for a job in the department store where her sister worked. At least, she reasoned, Margaret could afford to buy her own clothes instead of wearing hand-me-downs. "At night in the little personal hours I did the dreadful arithmetic," de Mille recalled. "Youth gone. No husband. No child. No achievement in work."

But de Mille would never give up dancing; she kept practicing, waiting for some event that would give her life direction. One February morning in 1942, she lay in bed staring at her telephone. Silently willing it to ring, she daydreamed about the calls she might get. Perhaps a Broadway producer would ask her to direct the dancing in his new musical. Maybe impresario Sol Hurok would offer her a series of concerts with her own company, or the Ballet Russe would ask her to take over as its head choreographer. The telephone finally rang. It was her mother, inviting her to come for dinner that night. She declined politely, then went out for breakfast.

Sipping coffee at a local drugstore, de Mille scanned the *New York Times*.

None of the news was good. The United States had entered World War II two months earlier, after the December 7, 1941, surprise Japanese attack on the U.S. naval base at Pearl Harbor, Hawaii. America's war in the Pacific was going badly; reports from Europe, where the conflict had been raging since 1939, were just as dark. London was reeling under relentless bombing attacks; Germany's Nazi armies controlled continental Europe from the Atlantic Ocean to the Volga River in the Soviet Union.

*Firebombed buildings surround St. Paul's cathedral during World War II. Reports of the Nazis' savage raids on London increased de Mille's gloom in 1942.*

Throughout the world, the Allies—Great Britain, the Soviet Union, and the United States—were retreating before the Axis powers—Germany, Italy, and Japan. Depressed by the war news, de Mille turned to John Martin's dance column, but it contained no encouraging reports, either.

De Mille returned to her apartment and gloomily contemplated the rest of the morning. "The choice before me was wide," she noted ironically. "For instance, I could make up a dance; or I could not make it up. If I did, would I ever get to perform it?" She put on a record and tried to create some new steps, but finally gave up and simply paced the floor. Her spirits lifted a bit in the afternoon, when she headed uptown for her dance class at Carnegie Hall. "There is always courage in a classroom," she said.

De Mille's ballet classes provided her with hours in which she could forget her disappointments and concentrate only on "the beloved floor, the classic empty floor."For a dancer, she observed in *And Promenade Home*, "floor space is as irresistible as cool waters to the thirsty. . . . No dancer comes out of a good practice without exhilaration."

The classroom also provided occasional comic relief. De Mille recalled the day when her temperamental ballet master threw out the piano player, claiming he could not keep time. The accompanist, who played for one dollar an hour, was Leonard Bernstein, later to become world famous as conductor of the New York Philharmonic Orchestra.

*Pianist Leonard Bernstein (above) lost his job with de Mille's dance class because, said the teacher, the future conductor of the New York Philharmonic could not keep time.*

When de Mille got home, her phone was ringing; it was Martha Graham, inviting her to a concert that evening. "Wear your prettiest dress," Graham commanded. "Walter Prude is coming." De Mille, in a "frisky" mood after her class, replied, "I don't wish to seem rude, but who the hell is Walter Prude?"

"Ah, you'll see," purred Graham.

Her curiosity piqued, de Mille donned a "slinky" black dress, pinned her hair up, applied extra mascara, and went off to meet Graham and Prude.

*De Mille chats with Martha Graham (left) at a theater party in the 1940s. When Graham arranged a blind date for de Mille in 1942, she changed her friend's life forever.*

Tall and slim, wearing impeccably tailored evening clothes, Walter Prude looked, recalled de Mille, like "a nice combination of [movie star] Gary Cooper and [King] George VI of England."

De Mille and Prude spent the rest of that evening—and every evening for two weeks afterward—together. He said he found her exhausting; she found him tantalizing. The two talked constantly—about "sex and the war and communism and other social amenities," de Mille recalled, and about themselves. The dancer learned that Prude, a college-educated Texan, had worked as a sailor and a secretary before joining the concert management firm that currently employed him. He loved classical music, had hiked through Europe, and, noted de Mille, "seemed to have none of the expected southern prejudices."

Walter Prude made de Mille laugh. "Laced through his polite manner, as brandy through milk," she wrote later, "was a savage wit." But, she added, "the predominating impression Walter made was one of gentleness, an instant and careful divining of hidden hurts and terrors. . . . And this is, I think, why he got on so well with artists and animals"—and, perhaps, why she fell deeply in love with him.

Two weeks after de Mille met him, Prude was drafted and sent to an army base in Biloxi, Mississippi. "Write me often," he told de Mille as he left. "Whether or not I answer, keep writing. This is important." Although he disliked public displays of affection, he kissed de Mille good-bye at the train station.

True to her word, de Mille sent Prude a steady stream of letters. Although she knew his knowledge of dancing was limited, she told him about her classes, about dressing-room gossip, about her efforts to find work as a choreographer. She also told him, she recalled later, about "all the lovely feeling of knowing who I was at last."

*Walter Prude (above) left for army service two weeks after he met Agnes de Mille, but he was already in love. So was de Mille. The pair married in 1943.*

The dancer's relationship with Prude had made her world a different place. She found herself more polite, more receptive to others: "People I met no longer seemed like animals trapped in the same cage," she said. De Mille also discovered she could concentrate on her work as never before: "When I thought about dance patterns, I kept my mind on them. Miraculously, I decided to stop failing because, briefly, I no longer had the taste for failure. . . . I could hardly recognize my mind. It was like a shiny new machine."

De Mille had always distrusted the idea of marriage, rejecting every potential suitor because she believed she could not have "dancing and true love at the same time." But as spring turned to summer in 1942, she began to think she could have both. In this frame of mind, she auditioned for and won a job as the choreographer and star of the Ballet Russe's new production, *Rodeo: The Courting at Burnt Ranch.*

The Ballet Russe contract called for de Mille to accompany the troupe to Los Angeles; there, she would choreograph and rehearse *Rodeo* between the company's summer performances. Receiving a first-class train ticket for the trip west, de Mille promptly exchanged it for cash and a coach seat. She would have to spend the five-day journey sitting up instead of traveling in a comfortable sleeping car, but she would have enough extra money to pay her rent. To avoid having to tip railroad porters, she packed her clothes in a wicker basket that she could carry herself. She planned to avoid the other dancers during the trip: "It would not do," she said, "for them to see their choreographer coming out of a coach!"

When *Rodeo* went into rehearsals, de Mille worked the dancers so hard that they could barely walk. For hour after straining hour, the men and women of the Ballet Russe unlearned most of what they knew, laboriously reshaping their movements to de Mille's specifications. After a summer of traveling and rehearsing up and down the West Coast, the company headed back to New York, where *Rodeo* would open in October.

Once again de Mille traded her first-class ticket for coach, this time so she could route her trip through Symrna, Tennessee, where Corporal Walter Prude was stationed. During their two-day reunion, de Mille danced all of *Rodeo* for Prude. "He thought it looked promising," she recalled in *Dance to the Piper*, "which was what I wanted to hear." When Prude's 48-hour leave ended, de Mille returned to New York and 3 weeks of final rehearsals for her new ballet.

Chaotic and triumphant, opening night ended with 22 curtain calls. De Mille needed a small army of stagehands to help her carry the bouquets sent by enraptured ballet fans. As soon as she could free herself from the throng of backstage well-wishers, she rushed to a telephone and called Prude. "*Rodeo*'s a smash hit! It's made a furor!" she shouted over the crackling long-distance wire. "I'm not surprised," Prude shouted back. "I knew it would."

Patrons leaving the Metropolitan Opera House were treated to the sight of celebrated theatrical producer Billy Rose stamping through the lobby and bellowing, "But where has she been? Why haven't we known about her? How could we have overlooked this talent?" *Rodeo* also impressed the critics. "As refreshing and as American as Mark Twain [author of *Tom Sawyer* and *Huckleberry Finn*]," said one review of *Rodeo*. "It is much the kind of ballet that Twain might have written if his mind had run to ballets."

*A glittering crowd packs New York City's Metropolitan Opera House, site of* Rodeo's *1942 premiere. When de Mille told Prude the show was a hit, he simply said, "I'm not surprised."*

*With Ballet Russe dancer Casimir Kokitch, de Mille executes a step she devised for* Rodeo. *"Why haven't we known about her!" screamed a noted producer after the show's opening.*

Equally intrigued was a trio of theatrical professionals who were working on a new musical, *Green Grow the Lilacs*. Composer Richard Rodgers, lyricist Oscar Hammerstein, and Theatre Guild executive Theresa Helburn saw de Mille as the ideal choreographer for their upcoming show, whose principal characters would be cowboys and their girlfriends. The day after *Rodeo*'s premiere, de Mille received a wire from Helburn: THINK YOUR WORK IS ENCHANTING. COME TALK TO US MONDAY.

De Mille resolved to be "firm and determined" in her talks with the *Green Grow the Lilacs* collaborators. She told them she would stage the show's dances, but only if she had absolute control over hiring dancers. "Oh, pshaw!" said Hammerstein to this extraordinary demand. But he was smiling. He believed de Mille to be the right person for the job; she, in turn, loved the songs he and Rodgers had written. Her demands met, the contract was signed, and rehearsals began.

The show—whose title was changed to *Oklahoma!* before its Broadway opening—examines the themes of jealousy and desire. Its story hinges on the relationships among Laurey, an attractive young woman; Curly, her handsome cowboy suitor; and Jud, a swaggering bully who wants Laurey for himself. When Laurey accepts Jud's invitation to a picnic, he suspects she only wants to make Curly jealous. Bitterly resentful, he plots Curly's death. All ends happily, with the joyful lovers united and the villainous Jud suitably foiled. Among the musical's songs were several that would become American standards: "Oh, What a Beautiful Mornin'," "People Will Say We're in Love," and the title song, "Oklahoma."

*Composer Richard Rodgers plays a few bars for his partner, lyricist Oscar Hammerstein II. The team's 1943 musical,* Oklahoma!, *made Broadway history.*

Before *Oklahoma!*, most musicals featured lavish production numbers that neither advanced the plot nor related to the characters. Rodgers and Hammerstein wanted to end *Oklahoma!*'s act 1 with a splashy circus dance totally unconnected to the story. De Mille wanted a ballet that would illustrate the characters' thoughts and emotions. "Finally," recalled de Mille later, "they gave me *carte blanche*. Dick [Rodgers] watched me like a hawk for three days. After the third day, he kissed me and said, 'Where have you been all my life, Agnes?' "

The result was *Oklahoma!*'s celebrated dream ballet. In this scene, Laurey, who has been trying to decide between Curly and Jud, sings "Out of My Dreams" as Curly appears onstage. Then dancers representing Laurey and Curly enter, the orchestra resumes the romantic strains of "Out of My Dreams," the actors vanish from the stage, and the ballet sequence begins.

Laurey, now played by the dancer, acts out her dream: She is about to marry Curly when the villainous Jud— also portrayed by a dancer—kills Curly and carries her away. At the end of the scene, actors replace their dancing counterparts. Jud shakes the sleeping Laurey awake and escorts her to the hoedown as the dejected Curly looks on. Laurey's emotions have been revealed to the audience through dance and pantomime rather than through speech. De Mille had transported the play from realism into fantasy and back to reality, telling viewers what the characters could not.

After weeks of frantic rehearsals and tense out-of-town previews, *Oklahoma!* opened in New York in the spring of 1943. De Mille, standing at the back of the theater, held her breath as the curtain went up to reveal a woman churning butter and a baritone singing about the beauty of a midwestern morning. As the song ended, the audience "gave an audible sigh and looked at each other," de Mille reported later. "They sat right back and opened their hearts. The show rolled."

When de Mille's "hocdown" number reached its conclusion, everyone—cast, crew, composers, and choreographers— knew something extraordinary was happening. Applause rocked the theater as composer Richard Rodgers shouted, "Oh, Agnes, I'm so proud of you!" Throwing her arms around his neck, de Mille said, "Dick, Dick, I love you." At that point, she recalled later, "the rehearsal accompanist started beating us on the back and shrieking, 'Will you two stop courting and look what's happened to the theater?' " Elegantly dressed first-nighters had leapt to their feet. "They were roaring. They were howling," recalled de Mille. "People hadn't seen girls and boys dance like this in so long!"

Reviewers soon trumpeted the news: Blockbuster hits Broadway! De Mille's poetic dance sequences and her sensitive use of American folk themes, said the critics, had revolutionized the musical theater. Playgoers mobbed the box office; tickets to the smash show would remain at a premium throughout its historic five-year run.

*Exhausted by de Mille's relentless rehearsals, a pair of* Oklahoma! *chorus dancers take a break between numbers.*

On opening night de Mille phoned Prude, by this time a lieutenant stationed in Omaha, Nebraska, and told him the show was a sensation. He congratulated her, then said, "When are you coming?" "Aren't you glad I'm a smash?" she asked. "Sure I'm glad," he responded. "When can you be here?"

Choreographers generally stay on hand to deal with problems that may crop up during the early run of a production, but de Mille abandoned *Oklahoma!* five days after it opened. She feared that the cast might resent her departure, but her anxiety proved unfounded. Her leading dancers saw her off at the train station with flowers, champagne, and broad grins.

De Mille and Prude spent their time together happily in spite of frequent long-distance calls from agents and producers. "I, who had spent hours and days in outer offices," she noted in *And Promenade Home*, "was now hunted down and searched out so that I could not have three uninterrupted hours with my guy." Nevertheless, Prude found time to say what he wanted to say: He asked de Mille to marry him. She burst into tears.

"In God's name, what's the matter?" he asked. "Surely this is not the first time anyone has asked you!"

"No," said the sobbing de Mille, "but it's the first time I've said yes."

Then, laughing and crying at the same time, she said, "There is some-thing you don't know about me: You haven't seen any of my work."

"But I'm marrying you," he said. "I'm not marrying your work." Then he put his arm around her and said gently, "I know what you want to do. That's the really important point."

When de Mille returned to New York, she immediately phoned Martha Graham and told her the news. "Yes," replied Graham calmly, "he told me a month ago."

"But he only asked me last week," de Mille said. "He took a lot for granted, I must say. I wish I'd refused him."

"Oh, yes, I know," said Graham. "Have you set a date?"

*A cowboy chorus serenades Laurey (wearing veil) in one of de Mille's most effective* Oklahoma! *dance sequences. The show, agreed critics, "revolutionized" the musical theater.*

*Aware that war will soon separate them, Agnes de Mille and Walter Prude wear somber faces in this photograph, taken just after their California wedding in June 1943.*

# SIX

# "Hot Property"

War-weary America took *Oklahoma!* to its heart. From Maine to California, jukeboxes and radio stations poured out the musical's bright, optimistic tunes; almost everybody could sing along with "Oh, What a Beautiful Mornin'" and "The Surrey with the Fringe on Top." Imitating Agnes de Mille's *Oklahoma!* dancers, women of all ages donned full-skirted gingham dresses and flowered straw hats, arranged their hair in topknots and ponytails, and exchanged their high heels for ballet slippers.

De Mille, who had once tried to will her telephone to ring, now found that it would not stop. On the line were calls from columnists, fashion writers, dancers, agents, investment firms, and producers. "Miss de Mille, I don't believe you realize what kind of a success *Oklahoma!* is," said a *New York Times*

reporter during one interview. "What kind is it?" asked the bewildered choreographer. "The biggest success," he replied, "that's ever occurred in the theater."

Snaking down West 44th Street, site of the St. James Theatre, a line of eager theater fans waited for a chance to buy tickets to *Oklahoma!* Most had to settle for dates months in the future. "I was invited out by people I had never heard of," recalled de Mille, "just in the hopes of cajoling tickets at any prices." And she found herself greeted with new respect at Sardi's restaurant, unofficial headquarters of the theatrical world. The year 1943, joked *Times* dance critic John Martin, had become "de Millennium."

*Oklahoma!* made de Mille famous, but it did not make her rich. Although the show's backers eventually earned

$30 for each dollar they had invested, de Mille's contract called for just $50 per week. "The bargain was hard," she noted, "but that is the essence of our theater—the hardest and sharpest bargain possible." De Mille could afford to be philosophical: Overnight, she had become a "hot property." Every producer on Broadway wanted to hire her.

Dick LaMarr, de Mille's newly acquired agent, urged her to live up to her star image: She should buy a mink coat, he said, hire a secretary, take taxis instead of subways. De Mille brushed off his suggestions. She already had a hand-me-down fur coat and, she sniffed, "I'd never in my life had a secretary." LaMarr said he could guarantee her $50,000 per year if she agreed to sign a long-term Hollywood contract. She declined. After waiting so long for success, she was determined to wait for the right project before committing herself.

"I liked as much money as I could get with no compromise, but I liked other things more," she explained. "You see," she told LaMarr, "either you believe I can only do it once or you believe that I have a real talent, and given a good chance, can repeat the success and maybe even do better. But I must be free to choose."

What she chose was an offer LaMarr brought her a few weeks later: the job of choreographer on a new musical called *One Touch of Venus*. "The people involved aren't exactly punks," LaMarr pointed out. They included some of the era's show-business giants: Kurt Weill, the German-born composer of

*Dance critic John Martin, whose* New York Times *columns had sometimes carped at de Mille, joined the cheering over* Oklahoma! *He called the year 1943 "de Millenium."*

*The Threepenny Opera;* celebrated American humorists Ogden Nash and S. J. Perelman; Elia Kazan, future director of the Oscar-winning film *On the Waterfront;* and Mary Martin, the musical-comedy star who would later appear in Rodgers and Hammerstein's *South Pacific* and delight millions of children with her portrayal of Peter Pan.

Rehearsals for *One Touch of Venus* would begin in August 1943. Prude and de Mille decided to hold their California wedding in June, when his next army leave fell. De Mille took her *Venus* advance—for once, a handsome sum—and bought herself a trousseau. Never particularly interested in clothes, she began acquiring them with delight. Her new garments, she recalled, "piled on my bed now, white on snowy white, ruffle on starched ruffle." Judging a traditional gown and veil inappropriate for a wartime wedding, she chose a brown suit to match her lieutenant's khaki uniform. Then she packed her bags and boarded a train for Hollywood.

Bride and groom met at the Los Angeles train station, bought their wedding license, shared a chocolate soda, picked up de Mille's father, and headed for the church. "We had nothing to say to one another," recalled de Mille. Everything had happened so quickly; were they, she wondered, doing the right thing? Prude thought so. "I've said I love you and that covers everything," he told his jittery fiancée. And when de Mille heard the wedding march, she knew exactly what to do: "As I'd done so often before camera or curtain," she recalled, "[I snapped] my fingers smartly. 'And!' I said as an upbeat and stepped out." Holding her father's arm, she proceeded toward the altar with her

*De Mille and composer Kurt Weill discuss their new show,* One Touch of Venus. *An instant hit in 1943,* Venus *has become a staple of the American musical theater.*

proud dancer's stride.

The couple spent their brief honeymoon at Prude's air base in New Mexico. All too soon, the time came for de Mille to return to work. Why, she asked herself, in the middle of a war, was she leaving her soldier husband to go plan a ballet? But she knew the answer: She and Prude had discussed the situation and made up their minds to be "realistic and practical." The choreographer had struggled for too many years to jeopardize her goals, which now lay within reach. Unless she returned to Broadway and once again demonstrated her abilities, her future would be limited. She had to prove she was capable of more than a single hit show. "Top *Oklahoma!* " advised one friend, "and you're fixed for life."

De Mille began casting the dancers for *One Touch of Venus* at the height of a blazingly hot New York City summer. Heat, she noted, is hard on dancers. "Their clothes soak through in an hour. . . . Hands drip and slip, making lifts dangerous as the girls slide like fish through the boys' insecure clutch. Feet blister." Nevertheless, when de Mille sent out a call for auditions, hundreds of eager young dancers flocked to the theater.

Selecting the female dancers proved relatively easy, but casting male dancers in wartime was another story. "The choice was paltry," de Mille recalled. "The U.S. Army and I saw eye to eye and they got first pick." Eventually, however, she lined up a cast of gifted dancers, all of them "fresh-looking and bright." Rehearsals began, marked by what de Mille called "traditional confusion and terror." Sets were a problem. Costumes were a problem. So were tempers, egos, exhaustion, strained backs, and twisted ankles.

One of the play's scenes contained a chorus of dancing nymphs. Proud of the outfits he had made for them, the costume designer dressed one of the dancers and called in de Mille. She almost fainted. "There seem to be breasts under her arms and on her back too," she said weakly. "That's the mysterious part," the designer responded. "You wouldn't want ordinary anatomy on nymphs surely!" The choreographer said this was exactly what she wanted; the designer threw down his scissors and stalked off in a huff.

The show's leading lady, too, presented a challenge. Mary Martin was a star but not a dancer. "She couldn't walk," recalled de Mille. "She couldn't stand. She couldn't raise an arm simply or directly." Martin, she said, "was sweet and eager and dear and pretty and a very real problem." But fortunately, Martin was also a trouper and a "great learner"; she eventually mastered her role to perfection.

Through the sweltering weeks of rehearsal, de Mille ached for her husband's company. "Nothing I do seems to have any meaning now except in relation to him. I only see and feel in order to tell him about it later," she said to one of the dancers. "I don't see how I can possibly stick it out for two and a half months." But stick it out she did, reaching opening night more or less intact.

*Stretching, primping, and leaping, de Mille's* One Touch of Venus *dancers surround the weary choreographer during the musical's final rehearsals.*

"I watched in sick panic at the back of the house," de Mille recalled. "When we got to the major ballet, I gripped the rail and prayed." But when the final curtain fell, the fear and tension that had consumed de Mille and her col- leagues had evaporated. Once again, Broadway magic had been made. *One Touch of Venus*, whose plot concerned an ancient statue of Venus that sud- denly comes to life in an American suburb, was a smash hit. The dances in

*Peering over a spray of white orchids from an admirer,* One Touch of Venus *star Mary Martin prepares to apply stage makeup in her theater dressing room.*

particular received ecstatic reviews. "My notices," de Mille reported proudly, "[were] much better than for *Oklahoma!*"

De Mille called her husband, now stationed in California, with the good news. "I'm glad you pulled it off, darling. Now for God's sake, hurry out," he said. "Our time may be limited." De Mille boarded the next westbound train. For the next few weeks, she and Prude happily camped out in a cramped boardinghouse room, the only accommodation he could find in the crowded army town. Then the dreaded call arrived: Prude had two hours to pack and ship out to a base in Missouri. From there, he expected to be sent to the European battleground. De Mille tried to look brave, but this time, her acting skills failed her. "Do you think you could manage to stop crying for a minute?" asked her husband. "I don't think so. No," she replied.

De Mille finally pulled herself together and accompanied Prude to the airport. "He kissed me once hard at the gate," she wrote afterward, "and then marched straight to the plane and entered without looking back." Silently, de Mille returned to the little room she had shared with her husband, gathered her belongings, and went to the train station. Back in New York, she received a comforting visit from her friend Martha Graham. "Hang on with all your hope," advised Graham. "You can, I believe, actually protect him. I feel this. I feel he will not be hurt." Then she added, "He loves you, you know." De Mille did know, but the days passed slowly without her man. "Two weeks after he'd gone," she said, "it seemed he'd been gone six months."

Coping with Prude's absence the only way she could, de Mille plunged into her work. While *One Touch of Venus* was still in rehearsal, the Ballet Theatre company had asked her to choreograph and star in a new piece, eventually called *Tally-Ho.* De Mille now went on the road with Ballet Theatre—America's first full-fledged classical dance company—traveling from New

*De Mille joins Ballet Theatre dancers in a Chicago rehearsal hall in 1943. Although the choreographer missed her soldier husband painfully, she believed that "work had to go on."*

York to Chicago to San Francisco, rehearsing her cast after performances.

The tour's frantic pace helped de Mille—and the other dancers with husbands and sweethearts at the front—deal with their worries and loneliness. "When we stopped to think, it seemed impossible to care whether a leg beat came on count 3 or count 4. And yet we had to care. Either we chucked everything . . . or we held together somehow the fabric of our lives," she recalled in *And Promenade Home*. "No purpose," she added firmly, "is served by accepting second-class work."

*Tally-Ho*, a comedic ballet, brought roars of laughter from the opening-night audience in New York. After the post-less room. On my pillow lay the lieutenant's card."

Like her fellow Americans, de Mille felt both hope and terror on June 6, 1944, when Allied armies launched their long-awaited invasion of Nazi-held Europe. Although Prude had been writing faithfully, military censors cut out all references to letter-writers' locations; de Mille had no idea where Prude was on D day. Nevertheless, she told herself, "work had to go on." When she was offered the job of choreographing the dances for a new Broadway show—*Bloomer Girl*, a musical set in the Civil War—she took it.

In *Bloomer Girl*, de Mille saw an opportunity to make a statement about living in wartime. She hoped to convey the feelings of women left at home while their men marched off to face death. Before she signed up for the show, she asked the producers if they would accept "a serious ballet about women's emotions in war." The producers said they would welcome such a dance. This show, they told her, would radiate "significance, seriousness, and poignancy." De Mille set to work.

The comic numbers fell into place smoothly, but de Mille ran into trouble with the big, emotional ballet she had in mind. After several false starts, she found herself barren of ideas. One evening the discouraged choreographer sat in the empty rehearsal hall with her friend Trude Rittman, the show's accompanist. "Not an idea presented itself. Not a gesture," she recalled in *And Promenade Home*. She began to think about her husband. "I wondered

*American dancer Lucia Chase and Anton Dolin—an Englishman who had changed his name from Sydney Francis Healey-Kaye—play a scene from de Mille's comedic 1943 ballet,* Tally-Ho.

performance celebration, de Mille's friends escorted the bone-weary dancer to her Greenwich Village studio. "I opened the door too tired to care longer and stopped dead still," she recalled later. "Beside the bed stood a young apple tree in full bloom, its arms spread out over the quilt, the blossoms pallid and clear and unmoving in the breath-

if he'd changed," she wrote. "If he would only walk into the room right now and put his arms around me. If I could look in his face again right now. Tonight. This night, in this dirty studio. In all this mess." De Mille described what happened next: "I found I was weeping very hard. I put out my hand to him."

Rittman said suddenly, "Aggie, what are you doing? Do that again. Get Jim [James Mitchell, the show's leading male dancer]. This is it."

When Mitchell received de Mille's call, he hurried to the studio. Together, he and de Mille blocked out a somber and moving ballet about a group of Civil War soldiers returning to their wives and families. De Mille knew that she had at last managed to capture her own anguish, her fear that she would never see her husband again. This dance, she suspected, was "something better than I had ever done before." But the show's producer and writers hated it. "Women will faint," said lyricist E. Y. Harburg. "They'll weep. They'll leave the theater."

"You don't know women," responded de Mille. "They'd rather have their grief talked about and shared than made light of."

Unconvinced, the producer vetoed the dance. "It's beautiful," he said, "but it's going to ruin our show." Finally, de Mille persuaded him to leave the num-

American troops stream toward France during the June 6, 1944, invasion that led to Allied victory in World War II. De Mille had no idea where her husband was on D day.

*Symbolizing the losses of war, a broken tree forms a backdrop for de Mille's dancers in* Bloomer Girl. *The choreographer felt a special commitment to the Civil War musical.*

ber in for the show's debut performance; after that, she promised, she would agree to its removal.

On opening night, de Mille watched from her usual spot at the back of the theater. "White-faced, the dancers performed with a tension that tightened the exchange between stage and audience to the point of agony," she reported. "Their gestures that night were absolute, their faces like lamps, and in the hush when Lidija Franklin [the female lead dancer] faced Mitchell, looked into her returned soldier's eyes and then covered her own because of what she saw, no one breathed. In the stillness around me several women bowed their heads."

At the end of the ballet, the audience sat in absolute silence for a moment, then burst into deafening cheers. By now, everyone loved the dance, even Harburg. At the post-opening party, he gave de Mille a hug. "To think a lousy bit of movement can make people weep, and me among them," he joked. "Darling," announced the producer, "it gives me great pleasure to state we were quite, quite wrong." Composer Harold Arlen offered a one-word opinion on the dance: "Hurrah!"

The homecoming ballet—which, predictably, stayed in the show—won unqualified critical and public approval and proved enduringly powerful. In the winter of 1944–45, New Yorkers and visiting out-of-towners battled for tickets to Broadway's biggest hits—*Oklahoma!*, *One Touch of Venus*, and *Bloomer Girl*—all of them choreographed by 39-year-old Agnes de Mille.

De Mille often told herself that, in spite of her successes, all she really wanted was a quiet life with her husband. "But deep in my heart," she confessed in *And Promenade Home*, "I knew I wanted nothing of the sort." Men, she noted, had always been able to enjoy both a home life and a career. Women, on the other hand, were subject to "greater emotional demands" and not expected to want both. Then, anticipating the thoughts of women a generation in the future, she said, "But I was in a new century and I was greedy. I wanted wifehood, motherhood, and work. I wanted all."

Kept from practicing the first two during the war years, de Mille concentrated on the third. When she was not rehearsing a show or planning a new dance, she could be found at army bases and hospitals, staging shows for wounded veterans and young men about to go into combat. She and her dancers, she recalled, felt "profoundly reassured" by their contact with the young military men. "Being with the soldiers," she said, "kept us somehow in a flesh-and-blood contact with all we believed in and loved."

In March 1945, Rodgers and Hammerstein started organizing a new show: *Carousel*, a musical based on Hungarian playwright Ferenc Molnár's drama *Liliom*. Hoping to repeat the success of *Bloomer Girl*, they asked de Mille to stage the show's dances. Molnár's 1909 play, a fantasy about a man who dies while committing a holdup, then returns to earth to settle his family's affairs, offered intriguing possibilities for a choreographer. De Mille took the assignment with pleasure and began to recruit her cast. First on her list was Bambi Linn, a gifted young dancer who had delighted audiences in *Oklahoma!*

The *Carousel* rehearsals proceeded normally—with tantrums, aching muscles, screaming battles, and tearful apologies. But when the show opened in New Haven, it fell flat on its face. Following a dismal first night, cast and crew went to work with surgical precision. Thrown out or drastically altered, recalled de Mille, were "the better part of act 2, half my ballet, five complete scenes, [and] a couple of good songs."

The revisions paid off: When the musical opened in New York, de Mille reported happily, "my protégée, Bambi Linn, stopped the show cold." At the conclusion of the *Carousel* ballet, the actors were unable to speak their lines over the audience's thunderous cheers. "This happens frequently in opera houses," de Mille pointed out, "but almost never in the commercial theater." Once again, she had scored an unqualified triumph.

Now the nation's number one choreographer, de Mille found herself flooded with offers from Broadway and Hollywood. But she had no desire to make any long-term commitments. The war in Europe had finally ended with the May 1945 victory of the Allies, and the choreographer hoped for a speedy re-union with her husband.

De Mille had not seen Prude, at this point stationed in Germany, for nearly two years. When a Hollywood producer offered her a contract to choreograph a movie, *London Town*, in England, she jumped at the chance. She knew military authorities would not permit her to go to Germany, but London was closer than New York; somehow, she and Prude would manage to get together. With her lawyer, she headed for the passport office to arrange for an exit visa from the United States.

As he made the usual requests for information, the passport clerk reached a crucial question. "Married?" he asked.

"As you see," de Mille replied, showing her wedding band.

"Husband's present whereabouts?" questioned the clerk.

De Mille responded, "U.S. Army overseas."

The clerk handed back her passport. "Go home, madam," he said. "We make no exceptions. You will not get permission to leave the United States."

Government regulations prohibited soldiers' wives from visiting their husbands overseas in wartime; although hostilities in Europe had ended, the United States was still at war with Japan. For the next two weeks, de Mille and her mother "pulled every possible wire," calling several U.S. senators, the British ambassador, and an acquaintance: Mamie Eisenhower, wife of the supreme commander of the Allied forces in Europe. The effort paid off; de

*De Mille sits for a 1945 portrait with a group of her favorite dancers. Seated at front left is Bambi Lynn, star of* Carousel; *at center right is* Bloomer Girl's *Lidija Franklin.*

Mille received her visa and flew to London on June 14, her second wedding anniversary.

De Mille had gotten herself to England, but not to her husband. She tried cabling and telephoning, but she had no specific address; letters to and from Prude had gone through the army post exchange. For all de Mille knew, her husband might have been sent back to the States or to the Pacific. Weeks passed without a word from him. She finally received a letter, but it contained crushing news: Prude's commanding officer, who disapproved of husbands and wives meeting in war-time, had delayed his furlough. It might be six months before he could make his way to England.

De Mille finished reading the letter in tears. Then the doorbell rang. Answering it, she found a soldier on the steps. He handed her a newspaper. "Your evening paper, madam," he said. It was Lieutenant Walter Prude. His furlough had been approved at the last minute. "I didn't do too much work in the next 12 days," reported the ecstatic de Mille.

After a joyful reunion, de Mille reconciled herself to Prude's departure. "After all," she told herself, "the shooting war was over and he was stationed less than 1,000 miles away, a near neighbor." Prude said he thought he could get another furlough three months later. By mid-August, however, he was aboard a U.S.-bound troopship. The United States had dropped two atomic bombs on Japan, bringing the global conflict to an end at last.

De Mille dutifully fulfilled her movie contract, but she was wild with impatience to get home. Not only was she stuck in England, she was trapped in a film she considered a disaster. (She later paid to have her name removed from its credits.) But when Prude called on her birthday, de Mille was bubbling with excitement and good news. "We're having a baby!" she shouted. "Good God! Are you sure?" he bellowed through the crackling transatlantic wire. Then the phone went dead. When Prude re-placed the call 25 minutes later, de Mille said, "Are you all right? Have you something to drink?" "A bottle of scotch," Prude replied happily. "I'm well along in it."

De Mille booked passage home on the *Empire Ettric*, a small freighter captured from the Germans early in the war. Just before she left England, Prude wired her with some good news of his own: He had gotten his army discharge and a job as assistant to impresario Sol Hurok. Immediately following Prude's cable was another, this one from Rodgers and Hammerstein. They were working on a new show, they said, and wanted de Mille to direct the entire production as well as choreograph it. This "was the first time a woman had been put in charge of a big Broadway musical," noted the proud de Mille. "It sent shivers of anticipation, pride, and uneasiness through my marrow."

As the *Empire Ettric* ploughed across the stormy Atlantic, de Mille paced the deck and considered her prospects. She and Prude had never really lived together; their meetings had seemed like a series of honeymoons. Now they were about to take up married life in earnest, and at the same time, learn to be parents. "What would that be like?" she wondered anxiously. "Would the baby distract me from him? Could I still dance?" Then, calming down, she envisioned a rosy future: "I could make notes for a book and—oh, yes—I could learn to cook. . . . Every night he would come home to dinner. The fire would be lit and I would be waiting and he would come home. All other problems and questions disappeared before this certainty."

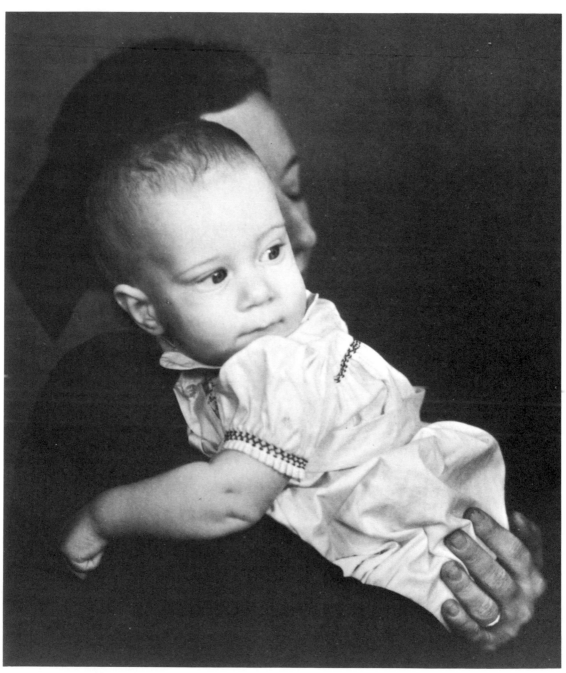

*De Mille hugs her son, Jonathan Prude, in 1946. A happy wife and proud mother, the choreographer was about to become the first woman to direct a major Broadway musical.*

# SEVEN

# New Horizons

De Mille's freighter steamed into New York harbor on a blustery November morning in 1945. From the deck, she scanned the jostling crowd on the pier, finally spotting her husband behind a row of uniformed guards. Port authorities announced that no one could board or leave the vessel until medical examiners had cleared the incoming travelers.

Prude's eyes met de Mille's. Ignoring guards and barricades, he strode to the ship's rail and took his wife's outstretched hand. "This is quite out of order," shouted a port official. "You must stop! You're not supposed to meet or touch until the regulations have been complied with." One of de Mille's shipmates, a kilted Scot, fixed the official with a fierce glare. "Mon," he said with a Sottish burr, "don't be absurrd!" At once, other husbands and

wives, some of whom had been separated since the war's beginning, rushed to follow Prude and de Mille's example. Now holding hands tightly, the pair just smiled.

De Mille and her husband settled easily into married life and, with the 1946 arrival of Jonathan de Mille Prude, into the role of proud parents. In 1947, de Mille hired an English nanny to help care for Jonathan and went to work on Rodgers and Hammerstein's new musical, *Allegro*.

De Mille staged the whole production on a bare floor, using back-wall slide projections as scenery. She employed the musical's huge cast, theater historian Ethan Mordden said later, "as if *Allegro* were a ballet for actors." The show, he added, suggested "the rural Americana at the core of [de Mille's] art."

*Ignoring the blistering heat of a New York summer, de Mille energetically instructs the dancers scheduled to appear in her upcoming musical,* Allegro.

Nevertheless, the new show failed to achieve the phenomenal popularity of *Oklahoma!* and *Carousel*. Adapted from earlier plays, these musicals were love stories set in bygone eras. *Allegro*, on the other hand, was an original work, its action taking place in the present and its plot more concerned with moral decisions than with romance. One observer called it "a problem show, weighed down with a mirthless, crackerbarrel book [script]." Its director-choreographer, however, received unanimous critical praise. "It is doubtful," said one theater observer, "that anyone but de Mille could have carried it off."

The choreographer's next work was *Brigadoon*, with words and music by Alan Jay Lerner and Frederick Loewe, the team later responsible for the 1956 Broadway hit *My Fair Lady*. A fantasy set in contemporary Scotland, the musical's plot concerns two young American men who discover an enchanted village in the Scottish hills. The village, Brigadoon, becomes visible to outsiders for only one day each century. One of the Americans falls in love with a young Brigadoon woman, but he must leave the village before nightfall, when it once again disappears. The young

man is heartbroken until the miracle of love makes Brigadoon—and his sweetheart—reappear before the allotted century passes. The lovers are reunited, and the American forsakes his own time to join the timeless world of Brigadoon.

To provide authenticity for her new work, de Mille studied Scottish folk dances. Her *Brigadoon* numbers included elements from the lively, graceful Highland fling and the intricate and difficult ceremonial sword dance of ancient Scotland. Dancer James Mitchell, one of the stars of *Bloomer Girl*, interpreted de Mille's choreography to perfection. His dexterity with the swords in the play's wedding scene, said one

*Holding a raised sword in each hand, dancer James Mitchell leads the cast of 1947's smash musical,* Brigadoon, *in a traditional Scottish dance.*

critic, made him "the envy of every hoofer on Broadway." An instant box-office smash, *Brigadoon* enjoyed a lengthy first run and numerous revivals. Eventually, it became part of the classic repertoire: Today, de Mille's dances for Brigadoon continue to be performed as a suite called *The Bitter Weird*.

But sorrow shadowed de Mille's *Brigadoon* triumph: Two days after the show's opening, Anna de Mille died of heart disease. For 42-year-old Agnes de Mille, the loss was devastating; she had always adored and depended upon her mother. She found some comfort, however, in knowing that her mother had seen her become the most successful choreographer in Broadway history, happily married and a devoted mother herself. On her deathbed, Anna de Mille read the *Brigadoon* reviews, the most glowing praise Agnes de Mille had yet received. As she had hoped to do, she had lived long enough to become known as "the mother of [her] daughter."

That daughter continued to make theatrical history. Between Broadway ventures, de Mille took choreographing assignments with Ballet Theatre (later known as American Ballet Theatre, or ABT). It was Ballet Theatre for which she created her modern-dance masterwork, *Fall River Legend*, a recounting of the infamous Lizzie Borden case.

The sensational Borden story began in Fall River, Massachusetts, in 1892. On the steamy morning of August 4, someone walked into the second-floor bedroom of 67-year-old Abby Borden

and smashed her skull with 19 blows of a hatchet. Soon afterward, the killer slipped into the downstairs sitting room and repeated the bloody act; Abby's husband, wealthy 70-year-old Andrew Borden, died from 10 hatchet blows to the head. Besides the victims, no one was known to be in the house at the time but a cleaning woman and the Bordens' unmarried 33-year-old daughter, Lizzie.

Arrested and tried for the murders, Lizzie Borden was acquitted 13 days later. The jury had been especially impressed by testimony that Borden was wearing a spotlessly clean dress when, only minutes after the murders, she discovered and reported the tragedy to the police. Borden, who inherited a fortune from her father, spent the rest of her life in Fall River, employing several servants and often contributing to local charities.

The Borden story gave rise to countless rumors, stories, and even poems. Generations of children skipped rope to a rhyme about the events:

> Lizzie Borden took an ax,
> And gave her mother forty whacks;
> When she saw what she had done,
> She gave her father forty-one.

Like many other Americans, Agnes de Mille found the Borden story fascinating; in late 1947, she began to study the "choreography" of the crime. After examining the floor plan of the Borden house and poring over police sketches and photographs of the victims, she concluded that an individual—Lizzie Borden, in this case—who wielded a hatchet over a victim would not neces-

*Walter Prude gives his son, Jonathan, a swimming lesson in 1947. Later that year, Jonathan's mother created her violent masterpiece,* Fall River Legend.

sarily stand in the path of the victim's blood. Thus, de Mille decided, Borden's spotless dress, the principal evidence of her innocence, proved nothing. She believed Lizzie Borden guilty of her parents' savage murder.

In *Fall River Legend*, de Mille presented her own version of the frightening story, recounting parts of the tale as they had probably occurred and fictionalizing others. The ballet, a powerful blend of modern and classical movements, portrays Borden—called "the Accused"—as guilty and examines her motives for murder. In the prologue, the Accused stands at the foot of the gallows as she listens to her murder indictment. Eight scenes follow, depicting the Accused's life from childhood to the time when she kills her parents; in the final scene, she turns to meet her own death on the gallows.

To dance the role of the Accused, de Mille chose 28-year-old Nora Kaye, an American ballerina who demonstrated both exquisite ballet technique and remarkable dramatic skill. A few days before the ballet's premiere, however, Kaye was taken ill, and Alicia Alonso stepped in. Born in Cuba in 1920, Alonso had earned a solid reputation for her romantic style and ability to interpret contemporary roles. She gave the performance of a lifetime as the Accused, a role she would often repeat in later years. (When Kaye recovered, she took over as the Accused, lending her own magic to the ballet.)

*Fall River Legend* opened in April 1948 to a mixed critical reception. Dismissed as "psychological nonsense" by

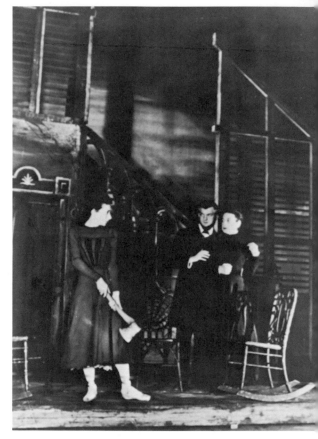

As the murderous Lizzie Borden, ballerina Nora Kaye stalks her terrified parents in de Mille's 1948 ballet, Fall River Legend.

one reviewer, it was hailed as "brilliant" by others. *New York Times* critic John Martin, by now known as the dean of American dance writers, raved about the new ballet. De Mille, he wrote, "has outdone herself in both the actual telling of the story and in the choreography in its individual scenes."

*Fall River Legend*, eventually recognized as a masterpiece, enjoyed numerous revivals; spotlighted during the

American Ballet Theatre's 25th anniversary gala in 1965, it opened in the Soviet Union in 1966. In her 1968 book, *Lizzie Borden: A Dance of Death*, de Mille commented on the Russian reaction to her ballet and its central figure: "On this tragic, Dostoevskian character, the Soviet people found a point of human relationship. This is an essential story, and although the officials claim that the troubles of one spinster are of no interest to a people pulling itself up to a better life, the people know better." Sellout Moscow audiences responded to *Fall River Legend* with loud, rhythmic hand clapping, the Russian equivalent of an American standing ovation.

In the years following *Fall River Legend*'s 1948 premiere, de Mille choreographed a string of successful Broadway shows. The first was *Gentlemen Prefer Blondes*, a 1949 musical adaptation of Anita Loos's best-selling comic novel of 1926. Playing Lorelei Lee, a mindless but lovable gold digger, actress Carol Channing stopped the show with "Diamonds Are a Girl's Best Friend," choreographed by de Mille in the jazzy, raucous style of the Roaring Twenties. Next came *Out of This World*. This 1950 musical featured words and music by Cole Porter, composer of *Nymph Errant*, the London show de Mille had choreographed in 1933.

The 1951 blockbuster *Paint Your Wagon* dealt with the California gold rush of 1849. Written by Lerner and Loewe, this splashy musical included several memorable de Mille dance numbers choreographed in her inimitable "Americana" style. The following year, de Mille staged the dances for *The Girl in Pink Tights*, starring French dancer Jeanmaire. A nostalgic musical, *Girl* was based on the making of *The Black Crook*, the New Jersey show de Mille had walked out on 25 years earlier.

*James Mitchell lofts dancer Gemze de Lappe during a love scene from* Paint Your Wagon, *the boisterous Lerner and Loewe musical de Mille choreographed in 1951.*

*Ballerina Gemze de Lappe prepares to board the bus that will carry members of the Agnes de Mille Dance Theater company across America in 1953.*

In 1953, the choreographer organized her own company, the Agnes de Mille Dance Theater. Traveling to 126 cities in 1953 and 1954, de Mille and her dancers introduced ballet to thousands of Americans who might never have discovered it otherwise. In the midst of her whirlwind activities, the choreographer found time to write. She published her first autobiographical work, *Dance to the Piper*, in 1952 and her second, *And Promenade Home*, in

1958. Offering revealing personal glimpses and intriguing tidbits from the dance world, both books became runaway best-sellers.

Always ready for new challenges, de Mille accepted a contract for a radically different type of show in 1961. It was *Kwamina*, a ballet set in an African colony on the eve of its independence. The choreographer, who had long admired the vigor and originality of African ceremonial dance, had used African dance motifs as early as 1940, in a piece called *Black Ritual*. Before beginning her new work, she spent months studying West African culture. When she finished, she had accomplished what she considered a breakthrough: introducing an American, predominantly white ballet audience to the authentic dance movements of black Africa. Fans and critics agreed: In 1961, *Kwamina* brought de Mille the theater world's most coveted trophy: an Antoinette Perry ("Tony") Award as best choreographer of the year. (The Tony was de Mille's second: *Brigadoon* had brought her the first in 1947.)

De Mille continued to create dances for American Ballet Theatre into the mid-1960s—*The Four Marys* and *The Wind in the Mountains* both appeared in 1965—but Broadway was undergoing a revolution. Absorbed with what came to be called the *counterculture*, audiences wanted experimental productions and rock operas, not the romantic musicals de Mille specialized in. The era's hit musicals included such youth-oriented shows as *Hair*, *Jesus Christ Superstar*, and *Godspell*.

As energetic as ever in her sixties, de Mille now concentrated on writing and on acting as spokesperson for the arts.

*Celebrating the 1952 publication of* Dance to the Piper *in a Manhattan bookstore, de Mille hands an autographed copy to her old London friend, choreographer Antony Tudor.*

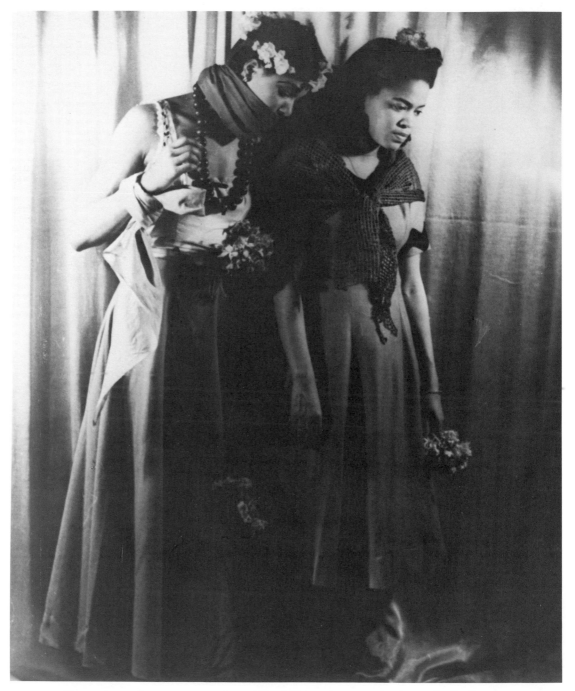

*Dancers perform a scene from* Black Ritual, *an early de Mille ballet for which she employed an all-black cast.*

*Teaching by example as always, de Mille works with Gemze de Lappe and Tommy Hall, members of the Agnes de Mille Dance Theater company.*

In 1962, she published *To a Young Dancer*, a handbook for dance students, parents, and teachers; in 1963, she wrote *The Book of the Dance*, a history of the art as she saw it; in 1968, she completed *Lizzie Borden: A Dance of Death*.

A towering figure in the theater world, de Mille exerted enormous influence; when she spoke, legislators listened. After hearing testimony from violinist Isaac Stern, producer Roger Stevens, de Mille, and other leading contributors to the arts, Congress appropriated funds to establish the National Endowment for the Arts (NEA). Organized in 1965, the NEA now dispenses about $170 million each year to artists and arts groups throughout the nation. De Mille served as an NEA committeewoman; she also worked for the National Advisory Committee for the Performing Arts, another body that supports arts-related projects.

De Mille had never forgotten the advice her friend Mary Austin gave her in 1927: "You must let the rhythm of the American earth come through what you do." In 1973, when she was 68 years old, the choreographer founded the Heritage Dance Theater at the North Carolina School of the Arts. Its goals include training young dancers and helping preserve traditional American dance forms. De Mille wanted to be sure that generations of future dancers would, as she had, feel the "rhythm of the American earth."

*Photographer Martha Swope catches de Mille in a pensive mood as the choreographer watches dancers rehearse for her 1970 ballet,* A Rose for Miss Emily.

# EIGHT

# Reprieve

Getting the Heritage Dance Theater on its feet proved to be slow going. In the early 1970s, most American patrons of the arts favored extremely modern, European-based work. They displayed little enthusiasm for traditional American dance or for de Mille's efforts to raise money to preserve and teach it. But by 1975, things were finally looking up: Several powerful institutions expressed interest in de Mille's project.

In May 1975, when the choreographer scheduled a lecture-concert, *Conversations About the Dance*, the Shubert and Rockefeller foundations, the board of International Business Machines, and the New York State Council on the Arts promised to send representatives. After the performance, to be held in New York City's Hunter College Playhouse, de Mille and her staff planned to mark the end of the Heritage Theater's financial troubles with a gala party. Thrilled by the prospect, de Mille looked forward to "an evening of celebration."

Shortly before curtain time, she gave her dancers their final instructions and attended to last-minute details. Then, handed a form to sign, she suddenly found herself unable to write. "My hand won't work," she told the cast in surprise. She soon realized she had no feeling at all on her right side. "Half of my body was dead," she recalled. "There was no pain, no sensation of any kind, no warning." Summoned by de Mille's alarmed associates, her doctor arrived minutes later. "Please do something fast," she told him, "because I've got to be on the stage in one hour delivering a very difficult lecture and I've never been late for anything in the theater in my life."

The doctor, she recalled, "looked at me very gently and quietly and said, 'You won't be on the stage and you will be late.' " He ordered his patient carried into a waiting ambulance. Theatrical to the bone, de Mille thought first of her dancers and her cherished project. "Right at that moment," she wrote in her 1981 book, *Reprieve*, "the life pattern of about 27 young people altered. . . . Together we were going to make the Heritage Theater a known and beautiful thing. Now they sat huddled in the auditorium like a clot of frightened children." After de Mille and her doctor left the theater, concert officials canceled the performance.

At New York Hospital, specialists quickly diagnosed de Mille, now almost 70 years old, as the victim of a massive stroke. The news spread quickly: Within the hour, TV and radio bulletins announced that the famed choreographer lay near death. "The *New York Times* had its obit ready," de Mille recalled. When her husband arrived at the hospital, doctors told him she would probably not survive the night.

As attendants eased de Mille into a hospital bed, she felt her mind growing cloudy and realized she was "talking funny." She recalled saying, "I am going to be bored, so terribly bored." But, she noted wryly in *Reprieve*, "I never said an untruer thing in my life. I was a lot of things in the near future, but I was not at any time bored."

For de Mille, the next few months brought a series of painful and confusing experiences. The first was a brain scan that revealed a life-threatening blood clot. "Walter seemed somehow standing near me, his face luminous with compassion," she recalled. Pitying her husband more than herself, she reflected: "He left behind at home that morning a perfectly sane woman, excited by the chance of success. . . . And now he found a depersonalized lump that could hardly babble her name."

The worst period of de Mille's illness, however, brought her an unexpected bounty: a strengthened bond of affection between her husband and her 29-year-old son. Jonathan de Mille, who lived in Cambridge, Massachusetts, had rushed to his mother's side as soon as he learned of her stroke. "My first vivid recollection," she wrote of the day she awoke in the hospital, "is of my two men, side by side, with their faces bent over me, their loving, dear faces, and I knew I was safe." Jonathan and his father, she noted in *Reprieve*, had never been "close and easy friends," but her stroke brought them together. "They have been deep friends ever since, deriving great pleasure and joy from their relationship," said de Mille. She credited her life to the new-found love between the two people she cared about most.

Thanks to the dedicated care of the hospital staff, to the constant, reassuring presence of the men she loved, and to her own indomitable spirit, de Mille survived the months of operations, therapy, and agonizing setbacks that

*The Pilobolus Dance Theater performs* Monkshood's Farewell *in the early 1970s. Intrigued by such experimental work, dance fans temporarily lost interest in traditional forms.*

*Heritage Dance Theater officials greet de Mille and her husband as the couple arrives at North Carolina's Raleigh-Durham airport in 1973.*

followed. Normally articulate and talkative, the choreographer found her speech difficulties—frequent in stroke victims—especially distressing. "For instance," she recalled, "a word like *campaign* might come out *pancake*. I believe this is a common confusion . . . but it's damned bewildering for both the speaker and the listener."

De Mille's mood varied between deep pessimism and characteristic optimism. Appalled by her inability to feel or control half her body, she "toyed with the idea" of suicide at one point.

But in the long run, she said in *Reprieve*, "I didn't kick against fate. . . . I did not say, 'Why me?' because the answer was so patently clear: 'Why not me?' I knew I was facing possible extinction, but I trusted not just yet."

Hoping to regain strength in her crippled limbs, de Mille began a grueling regimen of physical therapy. She approached her exercises with the determination of the trained dancer: Learning to walk again, she discovered, was much like learning to dance. And, she reasoned, if she had learned to dance at the relatively old age of 13, she could learn to walk again at the relatively young age of 69.

De Mille's visitors sometimes offered unwelcome sympathy: "How cruel because you are a dancer!" exclaimed one caller. "Nonsense!" snapped de Mille. "It's easier precisely because I was a dancer. I have submitted to discipline the whole of my life. . . . I learned patience that the ordinary nondancer never experiences." Grimly calling on that patience, de Mille made progress. "Little by little I learned," she recalled. "Little by little, very, very slowly."

Neurologist Fred Plum, who wrote the forward to *Reprieve*, gave de Mille credit for her own survival. Her recovery, he said, reflected "no passively received benefits of a modern 'medical miracle.' . . . [It was] the result of her own arduous efforts and refusal to be held down by mere physical handicaps." After three months in the hospital, Plum allowed his patient to go home on condition that she continue regular physical therapy. To help pass the long, slow days of convalescence, she began to work on a memoir of her childhood.

Unable to use her right hand, she taught herself to write with her left. Her memoir, *Where the Wings Grow*, provided its author with "another reason to hope." It did not matter, she said, "whether it was a good book or a bad book. It was my book and . . . there was a healing in all these memories." (Published three years later, the memoir received excellent reviews.)

De Mille wrote part of *Where the Wings Grow* at Merriewold, the summer home she had loved as a child. Keeping her company were her husband, their son Jonathan, and his girlfriend, Rosemary. One night at dinner, Jonathan announced that he and Rosemary planned to marry. De Mille, who loved Rosemary—she described her as "gentle-voiced, fresh as a rose"—later reported her reaction to the news: "I continued to munch stolidly as I al-

*Jonathan Prude, seen here with his mother in the late 1950s, reestablished his ties with his estranged father when the two met at de Mille's sickbed in 1975.*

ways do when moved." Her son asked if she was not surprised. "No," she replied. "I'm happy and delighted."

At the young couple's wedding the following November, bride and groom danced. Then, recalled de Mille, "Rosemary went into her father's arms and Jonathan should have taken me." But de Mille, of course, could not dance. "I was a dancer. I wanted to dance him proud," she wrote sadly. "Right then I grew old." Then she felt the presence of her husband. "I had the blessed experience," she recalled, "of rediscovering that the man that I had lived with for 32 years was in love with me."

Six months after her stroke, de Mille's doctors fitted her with a leg brace. "This gave me enormous freedom," she reported. Although she had always "despised the vogue for trousers," she now started wearing loose Chinese-style pants to conceal the brace. "Not that I was self-conscious

*President Gerald Ford presents the Medal of Freedom to de Mille's friend Martha Graham in 1976. First Lady Betty Ford had once been a member of Graham's dance troupe.*

about being a cripple," she noted with typical candor. "It was obvious that I was, and there was no use pretending that I wasn't."At this point, de Mille also blossomed out in vivid colors. "I threw away the blacks and the grays and the browns of middle age," she recalled, "and went hog-wild, indulging myself with the loveliest tunics and Indian Benares silk pants. . . . Another flag went up the mast to signal my recovering."

After another year of "recovering," spent completing her book, visiting friends, and attending plays and dance concerts with her husband, de Mille felt ready to travel. In October 1976, she agreed to attend a dinner party in Washington, D.C. The invitation came from President Gerald Ford; the occasion was a ceremony in which de Mille's friend Martha Graham would receive the Presidential Mcdal of Freedom, the nation's highest peacetime civilian award. The 83-year-old Graham, joked a pleased and impressed de Mille, would be "the first dancing girl ever to be granted such an honor."

With the aid of friends, a cane, and her leg brace, de Mille made it to the banquet, where she watched in delight as Ford decorated her old friend. But shortly after the ceremony, de Mille suffered a severe heart attack. Rushed to the hospital, she was met by her doctor, who ordered her admitted to the intensive-care unit at once. "I can't go home?" she asked plaintively. "I'm afraid not," replied the doctor. "Dammit!" roared de Mille. "That's what comes from having dinner with a Re-

publican!" ("Nobody laughed," she reported later.)

At de Mille's insistence, the hospital released no information to the press about her admittance. "Nobody should know I was sick again," said the exasperated choreographer. "It seemed I was getting to be a real bore, a redundancy. Again? Again, yet again? Yes-siree, over and over." Seventeen days later, her doctor's notes recorded, de Mille "went home, ready to resume her place in the dance."

Eager to start working again, de Mille approached Robert Joffrey, head of the Joffrey Ballet, with a proposition. Would he join forces in staging her production of *Conversations About the Dance*, the show that had been abruptly canceled by her stroke two years earlier? De Mille told Joffrey she envisioned "a big undertaking," involving a full orchestra and 40 dancers schooled in everything from classical ballet to square dancing. Such a huge project, said de Mille, would be "risky." Joffrey agreed that it would. He also agreed to do it.

Because she could no longer demonstrate her choreography, de Mille used rehearsal videotapes from the earlier production to instruct the Joffrey dancers. For those sequences not taped, she had to rely on written dance notations—which can only approximate movements—and on the memories of a few of the original performers. As rehearsals progressed, the company gradually mastered de Mille's choreography. "The dancers were very patient," she noted, "and we all learned together."

*Ballet stars Natalia Makarova and Mikhail Barishnikov flank de Mille during a 1983 tribute to the choreographer at Manhattan's Shubert Theatre.*

De Mille's return to work frightened her husband, whose memories of her stroke and heart attack remained all too vivid. "Why must you risk further?" he asked. "Walter suffered," admitted de Mille. "He was being asked to stand back and let me walk deliberately into danger, to risk incompetence, speechlessness, yes, even death—to gain what?"

Answering her own question, de Mille said, "It was not just another Broadway success but the sense of living and the rejoining of the active human race." She also knew the concert might represent her last chance to raise needed funds for the Heritage Dance Theater. The potential backers who had planned to attend the 1975 performance had promised to be on hand for this one too. "I felt I had to function the best way I knew how," said de Mille.

Fred Plum, de Mille's physician, agreed with her. "You cannot live your life as though you were going to die," he told her. "You will die, of course, and possibly sooner now than before. But you must live as though you will live. This is not a bad risk." De Mille's sister, critically ill with cancer, also encouraged her to go through with the show. Margaret, who would die the following spring, said, "Take your courage in your hands and do it."

De Mille discovered that working on the enormous show made her feel stronger. "I went to company rehearsals every day, promptly, and raised hell for two or three hours and went home and had my tea and slept," she recalled in *Reprieve*. "Whatever happened," she added, "this was to be my golden night! My resurrection."

On the night of the November 1977 performance, some 3,000 dance fans, foundation representatives, reporters, and de Mille supporters packed Manhattan's City Center Opera House. The curtain rose to reveal de Mille, resplendent in a brilliant red dress, standing with Robert Joffrey at stage right. A roar of applause swept the theater; de Mille sat down and started to talk. Rigid with tension at first, she soon realized that the audience was with her: "They intended that I succeed," she wrote later. "Never ever in my entire life had I experienced such support and caring from a body of people."

De Mille told jokes, shared her memories, discussed the history of dance in America, and introduced the performers as they illustrated her words with motion. For the show's finale, a boisterous square-dance number, de Mille played the part of the caller. When she shouted "Honor your partner!" she spontaneously extended *both* her arms, something she had not done for more than two years. Then, acknowledging a thunderous ovation, she faced the audience. "I had no cane," she recalled. "I had no support. I was alone out there, absolutely alone. . . . I stood without wobbling. I extended my arms again and the right arm did not waver. I held it high."

De Mille's "golden night" was followed by a shower of awards and accolades. She had already received the Handel Medallion, New York City's highest performing-arts award. In 1980, she accepted the Kennedy Center Achievement Award; in 1982, the Elizabeth Blackwell Award, which honors

*Surrounded by applauding dancers, de Mille takes a bow after a successful revival of her ballet,* Rodeo: The Courting at Burnt Ranch, *in 1980.*

*Walter Prude (above, in 1981), de Mille's beloved husband of 45 years, died in 1988 at the age of 79. The choreographer called her long marriage a "blessed experience."*

outstanding women in the arts and sciences. She published *Where the Wings Grow* in 1978 and *Reprieve* in 1981. *Oklahoma!*, complete with de Mille's choreography, enjoyed a smashingly successful Broadway revival in 1979.

Despite her burst of strength during *Conversations About the Dance*, de Mille never regained full use of her right side, continuing to rely on a leg brace and wheelchair. Refusing to let physical infirmities or advancing years slow her down, however, she kept on working for the causes she believed in. In 1986, for example, she appeared on a Public Broadcasting System special en-

titled "Agnes, the Indomitable de Mille." Responding to an interviewer's question, she said she wanted only one word on her tombstone: *Dancer*. But, she added quickly, she had no immediate plans for that tombstone: She was too busy working on her two new books and a new ballet.

Hoping to increase federal support for the arts, de Mille cohosted a Washington, D.C., party in May 1989. Rhode Island senator Claiborne Pell, one of the many political figures at the gathering, praised de Mille and her colleagues for their dedication to the arts and for bringing "the politicians and the artists in closer proximity to each other so that each side can see the other doesn't have tails and horns." The *New York Times*, reporting on de Mille's participation in the Washington gala, described her as "frail and sitting in a wheelchair, but seeming to be as alert as when she was choreographing for a generation of modern dancers." There was, added the *Times* account, "no doubt about Miss de Mille's . . . ability to win over the assembled congressional guests."

De Mille's "use of balletic choreography," noted author Robert Coe in his 1985 book, *Dance in America*, "changed the course of the American musical theater forever." *Oklahoma!*, the most successful Broadway show of the 20th century, has played around the world, with de Mille's choreography intact, almost continuously since it opened in 1943. The show owes its success not only to its entertainment value but to its place as a watershed in

*De Mille's* Oklahoma! *choreography lives on.* Above: *A 1979 Broadway revival of the musical, one of the most frequently performed shows in theatrical history.*

popular-dance performance. By incorporating traditional American dance forms with classical ballet movements, de Mille made serious dance accessible and enjoyable to a far wider audience than it had ever had.

In his *Broadway Babies*, author Ethan Mordden praised de Mille for her "artful blending of the musical's major elements—song, dance, and dialogue." Her "conceptual ballet," said Mordden, "solidified de Mille's hold on theatergoers' imagination. The best musicals needed her. . . . Put simply, she was the only one who did what she did." With "the emergence of de Mille," he added, "dance came into its own with . . . purity and clarity."

Through her works, de Mille has sought to attract an audience for dance that includes people from all walks of life. The success of her efforts has cre-

ated greater opportunities for dancers, enhancing their ability to make a living at the work they love. Perhaps even more important is the part de Mille has played in opening American eyes to the joys of dance. Her choreography and her writing have made countless readers aware of both the beauty of the art and the struggle that goes into creating it.

Praising "the radiance of her spirit" in his introduction to *Reprieve*, physician Fred Plum asserts that de Mille's example "is worth our examination, for those who can learn from and follow it will enrich their own lives as Agnes de Mille has enriched hers." Courageous, resourceful, absolutely determined to achieve the goals she set for herself, able to laugh at her own mistakes as well as to enjoy her successes, de Mille will be long remembered as an American original.

# FURTHER READING

Barnes, Clive. *Inside American Ballet Theatre*. New York: Hawthorn, 1977.

Coe, Robert. *Dance in America*. New York: Dutton, 1985.

De Mille, Agnes. *American Dances*. New York: Macmillan, 1981.

———. *And Promenade Home*. Jersey City, NJ: Plenum, 1980.

———. *Dance to the Piper*. New York: State Mutual Book and Periodical Service, 1987.

———. *Lizzie Borden: A Dance of Death*. Boston: Little, Brown, 1968.

———. *Reprieve*. New York: Doubleday, 1981.

———. *Speak to Me, Dance with Me*. Boston: Little, Brown, 1973.

———. *Where the Wings Grow*. New York: Doubleday, 1978.

Ewen, David. *Composers of the American Musical Theater*. New York: Dodd, Mead, 1968.

Maynard, Olga. *American Modern Dancers*. Boston: Little, Brown, 1965.

Mordden, Ethan. *Broadway Babies: The People Who Made the American Musical*. New York: Oxford University Press, 1983.

Rodgers, Richard, and Oscar Hammerstein. *Six Plays*. New York: The Modern Library, 1953.

# CHRONOLOGY

| | |
|---|---|
| 1905 | Agnes George de Mille is born in New York City |
| 1914 | Moves to Hollywood, California, with her family |
| 1918 | Begins dance lessons at the Kosloff School |
| 1923 | Enters the University of California at Los Angeles |
| 1927 | Graduates *cum laude*; parents divorce |
| 1932 | Gives dance recitals in France, Belgium, and England; remains in England to study with dancer Marie Rambert |
| 1933 | Choreographs Cole Porter's *Nymph Errant* |
| 1934 | Works with her uncle Cecil B. De Mille on his film *Cleopatra* |
| 1935 | Choreographs film version of Shakespeare's *Romeo and Juliet* |
| 1942 | Choreographs *Rodeo* for the Ballet Russe; begins work on Rodgers and Hammerstein's *Oklahoma!* |
| 1943 | Begins work on *One Touch of Venus* by Kurt Weill; marries Walter Prude |
| 1944 | Choreographs *Tally-Ho*, a comedic ballet, for Ballet Theatre and *Bloomer Girl*, a Broadway musical |
| 1945 | Choreographs *Carousel* |
| 1946 | Gives birth to a son, Jonathan de Mille Prude; begins work on Rodgers and Hammerstein's *Allegro* |
| 1947 | Choreographs *Brigadoon* |
| 1948 | Chorcographs *Fall River Legend* |
| 1949 | Choreographs *Gentlemen Prefer Blondes* |
| 1951 | Choreographs *Paint Your Wagon* |
| 1952 | Publishes first autobiography, *Dance to the Piper* |
| 1953 | Organizes the Agnes de Mille Dance Theater, which travels to 126 U.S. cities |
| 1958 | Publishes second autobiography, *And Promenade Home* |
| 1959 | Choregraphs *Juno* |
| 1961 | Wins Tony Award for Best Choreography for *Kwamina* |
| 1965 | Choreographs *The Four Marys* for American Ballet Theatre |
| 1968 | Publishes *Lizzie Borden: A Dance of Death* |
| 1973 | Founds the Heritage Dance Theater |
| 1975 | Suffers a stroke and is partially paralyzed |
| 1976 | Narrates *Conversations About the Dance*, a lecture-concert |
| 1978 | Publishes memoir of her childhood, *Where the Wings Grow* |
| 1980 | Receives Kennedy Center Achievement Award |
| 1981 | Publishes memoir of her illness, *Reprieve* |
| 1982 | Receives the Elizabeth Blackwell Award honoring outstanding women in the arts and sciences |
| 1986 | Appears on PBS documentary, ''Agnes, the Indomitable de Mille'' |
| 1989 | Cohosts a Washington, D.C., fund-raising gala for the arts |

# INDEX

# INDEX

# PICTURE CREDITS

Joan Beard, p. 22;   The Bettman Archive, pp. 19, 35, 46, 53, 55, 58, 59, 66, 77, 89, 97;   The Bettman Archive/Souichi Sunami, p. 32;   Culver Pictures, Inc., pp. 14, 63, 64, 71, 80;   Courtesy of Agnes de Mille, pp. 61, 87, 104;   Gjon Mili/Life Magazine © Time Inc., p. 73;   Barbara Morgan, p. 41;   Performing Arts Research Center, The New York Public Library at Lincoln Center, Astor, Lenox and Tilden Foundation, pp. 15, 17, 18, 20, 23, 26, 27, 28, 30, 31, 36, 37, 39, 42, 43, 47, 48, 49, 56, 60, 67, 68, 70, 76, 78, 82, 84, 85, 88, 90, 91, 93, 98, 99;   Performing Arts Research Center, The New York Public Library at Lincoln Center, Astor, Lenox and Tilden Foundation, © 1936 Metro-Goldwyn-Mayer Corporation Ren. 1963 Metro-Goldwyn-Mayer, Inc., p. 54;   Performing Arts Research Center, The New York Public Library at Lincoln Center, Astor, Lenox and Tilden Foundation/ Maurice Seymour, p. 12;   Performing Arts Research Center, The New York Public Library at Lincoln Center, Astor, Lenox and Tilden Foundation, Carl Van Vichten, p. 92;   Springer/Bettman Film Archive, frontispiece;   Martha Swope, pp. 94, 103, 105;   UPI/Bettman Newsphotos, pp. 24, 25, 34, 38, 44, 50, 51, 52, 62, 74, 75, 100, 102

Chelsea House extends its thanks to Agnes de Mille for her generous cooperation in the preparation of this book. The publisher also thanks Gloria Eustis of the Chester, Connecticut, Public Library for her valuable assistance.

Quotations from the following de Mille works are used by permission of Harold Ober Associates:

DANCE TO THE PIPER. Copyright © 1951, 1952, by Agnes de Mille. Copyright renewed 1979, 1980 by Agnes de Mille.

AND PROMENADE HOME. Copyright © 1956, 1957, 1958 by Agnes de Mille. Copyright renewed 1984, 1985, 1986 by Agnes de Mille.

SPEAK TO ME, DANCE WITH ME. Copyright © 1963 by Agnes de Mille.

REPRIEVE. Copyright © 1981 by Agnes de Mille.

**Margaret Speaker-Yuan,** who has lived in both Europe and the United States, holds two master's degrees: one in French from Claremont Graduate School, and the other in the humanities from Stanford University. Fluent in French, she works as a translator and free-lance writer. Her interest in dance began at the age of four, when she started taking ballet lessons after seeing a performance of *Cinderella.*

❖　　❖　　❖

**Matina S. Horner** is president of Radcliffe College and associate professor of psychology and social relations at Harvard University. She is best known for her studies of women's motivation, achievement, and personality development. Dr. Horner serves on several national boards and advisory councils, including those of the National Science Foundation, Time Inc., and the Women's Research and Education Institute. She earned her B.A. from Bryn Mawr College and Ph.D. from the University of Michigan, and holds honorary degrees from many colleges and universities, including Mount Holyoke, Smith, Tufts, and the University of Pennsylvania.